Eddie and I have known Dennis and Susan Wells since the early 2000s as well-known, active church leaders in South Carolina. Very few, if any, couples are ever as transparent as they, when it comes to life, marriage, and mistakes. This is one of the major reasons the book is so powerful ... Dennis and Susan have been through it! *The Intentional Marriage* peels away the myths that marriage partnership works only if it is 50/50, debunks the emotional dependency problems that end up creating anxiety and frustration, and the stupid words we all have heard, 'I fell out of love with him/her.' However, the most treasured part of their book is how the Wells rebuilt their marriage intentionally through gratefulness, trust, appreciation, time, worship, intimacy, and many other ways you will read about. Don't miss this opportunity to learn how to enhance your marriage. I did. I love this book. It's a must read.

Alice Smith
Executive Director
U.S. Prayer Center
Houston, Texas

THE
INTENTIONAL
MARRIAGE

*How a marriage made in Heaven
can work on Earth*

Dennis Wells, M.Min, MA, LPC

Susan Wells, MSPAS, PA-C

LIVING RIVER PRESS

Living River Press
Irmo, SC 29063
803-318-5400

ISBN: 978-0-9910310-0-9
Printed in the United States of America
First Printing 2013.

Unless otherwise indicated, all Scripture quotations are taken from the Holy Bible, New Living Translation, copyright © 1996, 2004, 2007 by Tyndale House Foundation. Used with permission. All rights reserved.

Scripture quotations taken from the New American Standard Bible®, Copyright © 1960, 1962, 1963, 1968, 1971, 1972, 1973, 1975, 1977, 1995 by The Lockman Foundation Used by permission." (www.Lockman.org)

Scripture taken from the New King James Version®. Copyright © 1982 by Thomas Nelson, Inc. Used by permission. All rights reserved.

Scripture quotations are from The Holy Bible, English Standard Version® (ESV®), copyright © 2001 by Crossway, a publishing ministry of Good News Publishers. Used by permission. All rights reserved.

Scripture quotations marked (NIV) are taken from the Holy Bible, New International Version®, NIV®. Copyright © 1973, 1978, 1984, 2011 by Biblica, Inc.™ Used by permission of Zondervan. All rights reserved worldwide. www.zondervan.com The "NIV" and "New International Version" are trademarks registered in the United States Patent and Trademark Office by Biblica, Inc.™

Editing by Lori Hatcher
Layout by William Baker Design

DEDICATION

To our children, Daniel, Mary Catherine, and Anna—thank you
for your love and prayers as we walked this journey. Our prayer is
for you and your spouses to have intentional marriages that exceed
your wildest dreams.

CONTENTS

ACKNOWLEDGMENTS

We are grateful to the many people who helped bring this book to print. Our first acknowledgement of gratitude goes to our Heavenly Father for healing, restoration, and redemption.

We're also thankful for our parents: Herbert and Jean Wells (Mom is now with Jesus) and Ted and Ann Bailey as examples of faithfulness to each other. We're thankful for the friends (you know who you are) who have cried and laughed with us, held us accountable, and encouraged us to put our experiences into print.

And finally, we're thankful for our wonderful editor, Lori Hatcher, whose relentless work brought clarity to our passionate words and assisted us in birthing this book. We are blessed, and we know it.

FOREWORD

Dennis and Susan Wells looked like a model couple when I first met them in 1997. They seemed genuinely happy. I admired their love for each other. They were pastors, so I knew the pressures of ministry were overwhelming. But they were obviously in love with each other, and they had wonderful children.

I never would have predicted that a few years later their marriage would unravel. But that's exactly what happened.

I'll never forget the phone call I received from Dennis in 2001. We'd become close friends, but I felt helpless when I learned that he and Susan were in big trouble. Their storybook romance was falling apart because of unfaithfulness. There was nothing I could say or do that could bring them back together. A dark abyss of miscommunication, unmet needs, unrealistic expectations and hurtful words could be found under the veneer of their ideal Christian marriage.

When the painful truth came out, Dennis and Susan abruptly separated. They and their kids were hit by a tsunami of shame and grief. It was compounded by the fact that not all the Christians they knew reached out to help. As is often the case, the trauma of a marriage breakup was compounded by judgments, aloofness and loneliness.

That's how a lot of marriages end. Many men and women today—including too many Christians—just let sin and selfishness take its course. That's why the divorce rate has skyrocketed in recent years. It ends up being the easy solution even though divorce leaves unimaginable heartache in its wake.

Thankfully Dennis and Susan's story didn't end in divorce court. God performed a miracle, and what seemed dead came to life again.

Just as Jesus brought Lazarus out of a tomb after four days, He called Dennis and Susan's marriage out of darkness and performed a resurrection. It didn't happen instantaneously—and it wasn't without fits and stops—but it is still nothing short of supernatural. Anybody who knows Dennis and Susan today will realize that God can totally heal broken relationships.

Dennis and Susan don't justify the mistakes they made. In fact they are brutally honest about them. But now they realize that God can completely restore a marriage that has been ripped apart by adultery. And because they learned from their mistakes, they are able to share about their failures with others so they can avoid the same pitfalls.

This excellent book reminds readers that married couples must be intentional if they expect to preserve and protect their marriage bond. After the initial shock of the affair that tore Dennis and Susan apart, they allowed God to heal their hearts to the point that they could communicate again. They were intentional about taking the needed steps to reconcile.

Today, their bond is stronger than ever—and they can tell you that their love is deeper. On their journey to healing they learned amazing lessons about communication, forgiveness, covenant and kindness. And now they are sharing those lessons with all of us.

Regardless of the status of your marriage—whether it is happy and stable or on the verge of collapse—this book will help you. I encourage you to open your hearts and let Dennis and Susan coach you on the path to transformation. My prayer is that the miracle that happened in their troubled marriage will be repeated thousands and thousands of times.

J. Lee Grady
Author of *The Holy Spirit Is Not for Sale* and *Fearless Daughters of the Bible*

INTRODUCTION

The year 2001 was a year of extreme highs and lows. For the past seven years, Susan and I had been working to revitalize a dying church. We began with only five people, but our church was growing, and we had just completed a major remodeling project. After seven years of plowing and planting, we enjoyed a week of special services to celebrate our new sanctuary. Our body of believers was finally becoming all we had envisioned.

Then came September 11—the day of the worst terrorist attack on U.S. soil. When the Twin Towers in New York crumbled to the ground, our country's way of life changed forever.

In October, Susan and I experienced our own personal tragedy. An extramarital affair caused the twin towers of our family and ministry to crumble to the ground, and our family's life changed forever. After the initial shock and numbness, there was fallout—hurt, tears, questions, and many sleepless nights. We separated for 19 months, and our children divided their time between our two households.

Never-ending questions dogged our days and haunted our nights. *Can this relationship be repaired? Does either one of us want the relationship to be repaired? Is divorce unavoidable?* Even some of our closest friends encouraged us to cut our losses and move on.

Those outside our immediate family suffered as well—our beloved church could no longer bear up under the weight of our personal struggles. When visitors came, there were no easy answers for where the pastor's wife was. Nine months after Susan and I separated, our church leadership voted to close the doors. This was a humbling and devastating process.

Meanwhile, Susan and I began searching for answers. Months of individual and joint counseling sessions began to shed light on where we went wrong. We earnestly sought to mend our ways and seek new ways of living with each other. We discovered and began to understand how faulty conflict resolution and feelings of worthlessness had eroded the foundation of our relationship. With the help of courageous counselors, we learned new methods for handling old issues.

We are forever grateful for the friends who did not treat us like lepers and for the counselors who bravely walked with us through the storm.

God's grace was abundant—He gave us a second chance to live as husband and wife. Almost two years after the affair, on our wedding anniversary, we renewed our vows to each other while our children and friends watched with joy.

The work didn't end, however, with that very special service. This was just the beginning of a new journey as we talked, listened, shared real and raw feelings, and continued to forgive. We learned the importance of being intentional in every area of our marriage and our lives.

We know now that life is meant to be lived intentionally. Without intentionality, we find ourselves tossed from one crisis to another without any way to correct our course. This inability is magnified when we enter into a relationship with another. Most couples suffer from the misconception that when two people come together under the umbrella of marriage, their relationship becomes a beautiful thing all by itself. Unfortunately, there's no such thing as an auto-pilot for relationships.

The truth is that two people, from two different backgrounds, with baggage from other relationships or dysfunctional families, will struggle to do life together. This truth is a little scarier than the fairy tale picture of most wedding plans. The good news is that we can learn new ways to approach relationships and marriage.

This book was born out of our own personal journey and has been field tested in our own relationship. Because we know the material works, we've been eagerly sharing it in marriage seminars since 2011. For more information about hosting a seminar for your group, please visit our webpage: http://www.theintentionalmarriage.net.

What we share here are very practical ways to have a committed and loving relationship. Instead of being haphazard in our every interaction, we can choose to be intentional.

Recently, we took our first trip to New York City. While we were there, we made a point to visit the 9/11 Memorial. After a somber time of viewing the two pools set in the footprints of the original Twin Towers, reading the names of the victims, and reflecting on the events of that day, we made our way through the many trees that stood on the plaza. One tree caught our eyes. We noticed that it didn't match the hundreds of others. A small fence surrounded it, and its shape was different.

After consulting the 9/11 brochure, we realized this tree was the "Survivor Tree"—the only tree to survive in the wreckage at Ground Zero despite being reduced to an eight-foot-tall stump. The tree was nursed back to health and now stands 30 feet tall, sprouting new branches and flowering in the springtime.

As we read its history, Susan and I were overwhelmed with emotion. We realized that while this tree symbolizes the healing and restoration that has taken place in New York City, it also parallels the healing, restoration, and new life God has brought to our marriage.

Dennis & Susan
in front of the
"Survivor Tree"

CHAPTER I

MARRIAGE MYTHS

DISPELLING MARRIAGE MYTHS

Like many things in life, myths have a way of masquerading as truth. If we hear something often enough, we tend to believe it. Sometimes, what we see on TV or the internet becomes part of our belief system. We jokingly say, "If it's on the Internet, it must be true." Movies also powerfully influence us. We watch Hollywood's version of relationships and believe this is what our own should look like. The drama, sappy dialogue, and perfect sunsets all feed our belief that a relationship must be perfect to be right.

Over the years we've swallowed many myths about marriage and relationships. Let's look at a few:

I FELL IN/OUT OF LOVE

How many times have you heard this explanation for why someone is either in or out of a relationship? I (Dennis) have often heard an adulterous spouse use these words to describe how he became involved with another person. "We didn't mean for it to happen," he says, "It just did."

Sometimes a spouse decides it's time to move on to someone new, and she says, "I just fell out of love."

Let me say up front—we don't fall in or out of love. Love is not an accident. It's not a pothole we miss and accidentally fall into. And it's not a boat on the ocean we accidentally fall out of.

Love also doesn't sneak up on us.

Love at first sight is not accurate. We may have an attraction or interest at first sight, or we may feel sexual attraction when we first meet someone, but it's not love.

Love takes time. Love is developed. Love is a choice.

Falling in love is a subtle process. As we invest time in our relationship, we bond with each other. Wherever we invest our time, energy, and emotions, we see a return. If we invest time, energy, and emotion into our spouses by spending time together in quality activities, we see our love grow.

Love takes time.
Love is developed.
Love is a choice.

Falling out of love is also a slow process. It might not be deliberate or intentional, but's never a sudden event. It happens over time. Sometimes we fall out of love because we've unintentionally neglected our relationship. Like many things in life, (gaining weight, for example), the changes happen so subtly we don't even notice until our relationship is in deep trouble.

The term *falling out of love* is more accurately stated *sliding out of love*. While this slide happens over the course of time, there's usually a point where we begin to entertain the idea of being involved with another person. Sometimes spending time with a coworker in the business trenches and the "heat of the battle" at work can cause us to become attracted to someone else. This causes us to loosen our morals and values and begin to consider the possibility of another relationship.

YOU COMPLETE ME

We've all heard this sappy Hollywood line in a movie or read it in a cheap greeting card. On the surface, it sounds very romantic. The thoughts behind it are:

My life was empty until you came along.
Until you, I had no meaning.

I was missing the part that makes me a whole being.

When we say this, what we're really saying is that God created us incomplete, and the only way we can be whole is to find someone to complete us. If we buy into this lie, we spend our lives looking for someone to fill the holes. This belief often causes two very unattractive character traits—neediness and desperation.

We must be able to stand alone before we can have a healthy relationship with someone else. If we're self-sufficient emotionally, we stand a better chance at having a healthy relationship that doesn't emotionally deplete another person. To have the best chance at a healthy relationship, we should seek a union with someone who is self-sustaining and emotionally secure.

It's important to note the difference between *needing* to be with someone and *choosing* to be with someone—enjoying each other's companionship without feeling *compelled* to be with them.

A healthy posture is this: You may enhance or add to my life, but I don't need you. I can be complete without you.

MARRIAGE IS 50/50

When we say marriage is 50/50, what we mean is *I bring 50 percent into the relationship, and you bring 50 percent*—like splicing two halves together. In biology, this usually creates a monster.

When we hold back and bring only half of ourselves into a marriage, what happens to the other 50 percent? It often presents itself as selfishness. While we never say it aloud, it manifests itself in our actions. It's a constant struggle to maintain what's mine. One symptom of this mentality is the tendency to have frequent arguments about what's fair.

A 50/50 relationship means that each person has one foot in and one foot out. We choose to limit our involvement rather than be all in. This hesitancy to commit is rooted in a fear that pledging 100 percent of ourselves might be dangerous or detrimental.

It's important to remember that marriages are unions, not orga-

18

nizations. It's ok, even healthy, to decide to commit only a certain percentage of ourselves to an organization. It's not ok, however, to bring anything less than 100 percent into our marriages. The only way a marriage can thrive is if both partners are all in.

WE GREW APART

This statement is also rooted in a lie. It implies that we have no control over the direction in which we are growing in our relationship.

Susan and I planted a willow tree in our back yard several years ago. After a few months, we noticed the tree was bending toward the sunny spot in our yard. Instead of growing straight and tall, the tree was leaning awkwardly to one side.

To correct this, I tied a piece of rope to the trunk of the tree and anchored the other end to the fence. This corrected the tree's growth, and before long its trunk and branches were straight and healthy again.

Like my tree was starving for sunlight, our marriages also suffer from lack of nourishment. Failing to spend time together will cause gaps. It may be as subtle as becoming consumed with our work. We might spend more and more time at the office so we can get ahead. Or we may be obsessed with a new hobby and spend all our free time and money on "me" time.

Failing to spend time together will cause gaps.

Working hard at our jobs and enjoying hobbies are not bad things, but if we give the best part of ourselves to anything other than God and our families, we'll notice gaps developing in our relationships.

We often interpret these gaps as growing apart, when in reality, they are only symptoms to alert us to the need for a course adjustment. Like I took corrective measures to ensure that my tree grew in a healthy way, we can close the gaps in our marriages by taking steps to grow together.

We must be intentional about cultivating and discovering activities and interests we can enjoy together. It's not healthy to spend every waking moment with each other, or always do everything together (we'll discuss this later), but it is important to make our relationship a priority.

Growing apart happens over time, but the good news is that growing together can happen the same way. It will, however, take the intentional efforts of both parties to make it happen.

Remember—myths are not the truth. Just because you see it on the internet, TV, or movies doesn't make it true.

CHAPTER 2

BE INTENTIONAL ABOUT...

PROTECTING YOUR MARRIAGE

Marriage was God's plan. The whole concept originated in the mind of our wonderful Creator. It's obvious the human mind isn't capable of designing something so incredible, wonderful, beautiful, wise, and sovereign.

We see the beauty and wisdom of God's plan for marriage in Ephesians 5, where Paul dedicates a significant portion of the letter to a the dynamics of the husband/wife relationship. As we study this and other passages of the Bible contained here and in Chapter 6, I've included definitions in parenthesis following each significant word. These definitions are from Strong's Exhaustive Concordance of the Bible.[1]

In Ephesians 5:32, Paul reveals,

> *"This is a great mystery, but it is an illustration of the way Christ and the church are one."* (NLT).

Here we see that God's intent from the beginning was to use marriage as a visual illustration of His relationship with His church. It was, and still is, a *beautiful plan.* In Genesis 1:26-28, we read:

"Then God said, 'Let Us make man in Our image (likeness, resemblance) *according to Our likeness'...*

"God created (to shape/fashion with God as the subject) *man in His own image, in the image of God He created him; male and female He created them.*

"God blessed them; and God said to them, 'Be fruitful (bear fruit) and multiply (become/grow great, increase), and fill (have fullness, abundance; be accomplished; be armed; be satisfied; complete) the earth (land, territory, region, land of Canaan), and subdue (subject, dominate, tread down) it; and rule (have dominion, tread down) over the fish of the sea and over the birds of the sky and over every living thing that moves on the earth.'" (NASB)

We see more of God's beautiful plan in Genesis 2:15: "The Lord God TOOK the man and PUT him in the GARDEN of EDEN to CULTIVATE and KEEP it." (NASB) Understanding the original meaning of the capitalized words in this passage helps us see more clearly the heart of God for mankind in marriage and understand his blueprint for a successful marriage.

God's perfect plan is for each individual to be married to the Lord before they are married to each other.

TOOK

First, God took Adam. He laid hold of him and received him, very much like a man *takes* a wife in order to marry her. It's important to realize that God initiated the relationship with Adam. He didn't just create him and dump him in the garden with the command, "Come find Me if you can!"

Romans 5:8 also testifies to how God initiated a relationship with mankind: "But God showed his great love for us by sending Christ to die for us while we were still sinners" (NLT). Before we knew God, He demonstrated His love to us, filthy sinners, through the death of His Son, Jesus, on our behalf. Remember, God is always the initiator. Having a relationship with Him is an essential part of a healthy marriage.

God's perfect plan is for each individual to be married to the Lord *before* they are married to each other. This is a crucial first step in establishing a healthy, *intentional* marriage.

PUT

Next, God put Adam in his assignment. The word *put* means "to rest, settle down and remain; make quiet." God's design for marriage is that it should be a relationship of rest and quiet, a safe place to "settle down and remain."

Here's a question every couple should answer:

What things/people/activities generate strife and unnecessary "noise" or create an unsettled atmosphere in our marriages that make us want to run and escape?

Talk about the answer(s) to this question and, if necessary, eliminate these noise-producing elements from your lives.

God expands on the meaning of *put* (to settle in a relationship of rest and quiet) in Proverbs 31:11 (NKJV):

"The heart of her husband safely trusts her."

If we as women are in right relationship with God and our husbands, everything we do will foster an attitude of trust. This is should be our goal. Because men deeply desire a safe place for their hearts, this is KEY. Men crave places of rest and quiet. Because men battle so much outside their homes, in the work environment and in other relationships, they want their relationships with their wives to be characterized by minimal battles and maximum peace.

And husbands, lest you think you're off the hook, God directs I Peter 3:7 to you: *"In the same way, you husbands must give honor to your wives. Treat your wife with understanding as you live together. She may be weaker than you are, but she is your equal partner in God's gift of new life. Treat her as you should so your prayers will not be hindered"* (NLT).

A husband who seeks to understand his wife demonstrates that he values her.

Women want to be understood, or at least know their husbands are trying to understand them. This provides the *safe place* of security women crave. A husband who seeks to understand his wife demonstrates that he values her.

THE GARDEN

God placed the first husband and wife in the Garden. The word *garden* speaks of an "enclosure; enclosed garden." For marriage to be a "garden," it *must* be enclosed.

In a marriage garden, two things come to mind: First, there's only room for two—one man and one woman. Second, there must be boundaries. No person, place, or thing should be allowed to come between a husband and a wife. This includes family members, friends, hobbies, ministry, job, etc.

As we have children and become a family, it's important to remember that we were *couples* before we were *parents*. We must maintain our identity as a couple, especially in light of the demands and responsibility of rearing children.

One day our children will grow up and leave home, and we'll be left alone. Will we know what to do with each other? Our spouses can and should be our best friends, but this can only be true if we make and keep our relationship a priority.

A couple should never allow their extended family to come between them.

It's also important to realize that our marital boundaries must include our "in-loves." When a man marries, God commands him to leave his father and mother and cleave to his wife. While God specifically directed this instruction to men, it applies to both the husband and the wife. A couple should never allow their extended family to come between them. This doesn't mean disassociating with our extended family; it means establishing boundaries and communicating them in a Christ-like, respectful manner.

EDEN

The word Eden is defined as "pleasure; delight oneself." Now take a deep breath, let it out slowly, and SMILE … God is OK with us enjoying the *pleasure* of marriage. In fact, sex is His idea. It is God's wedding present to the bride and groom, and it's meant to be *delightful.* In addition to bringing pleasure to our lives, it's also a mighty weapon of warfare to protect our marriage. Paul speaks of this in I Corinthians 7:5:

"Stop depriving one another, except by agreement for a time, so that you may

devote yourselves to prayer, and come together again so that Satan will not tempt you because of your lack of self-control." (NASB)

Do you know we actually protect our marriages when we have, in addition to the other components of a healthy marriage, an active, vibrant sex life? This is yet another reason to praise God.

CULTIVATE AND KEEP

This section would be incomplete if we didn't address the fact that having an intentional marriage involves the four-letter word W-O-R-K. There's just no way around it. The two assignments God gave Adam and Eve, the first husband and wife, were to cultivate and keep the Garden of Eden. As we compare our marriages to God's example of life in the Garden of Eden, we see some important parallels.

The word *cultivate* means "to work, serve, work for another, serve another by labor; till the land." This sure sounds like work. Just like a garden doesn't till, sow, weed, or harvest itself, neither does a marriage. We must not allow the ground of our marriage to become fallow. Fallow ground is plowed, but left unseeded for a season or more.

One of the best ways to successfully accomplish this cultivation is to perform small acts and words of kindness and gentleness— doing and saying things that convey we value each another. We can do this by working as partners in the home and with the kids and praying for and with each other. In these ways, we demonstrate that we honor one other.

To fully understand the job description God gave Adam and Eve, we must understand what the word *keep* means. Its most accurate definition is "to keep guard, observe, have charge of, keep watch, protect, and be one's guard." This implies that what is being kept is valuable and therefore requires protection. Remember that marriage was the first institution the Lord created. Because it manifests His kingdom plan for creation, it will always be under attack. We're

We must not allow the ground of our marriage to become fallow.

25

not, however, at a disadvantage. God's Word is filled with promises about the warfare and weaponry we can use to defend our marriages. These include:

II Cor. 10:4 — *"For the weapons of our warfare are not carnal but mighty in God for pulling down strongholds."* (NKJV) Carnal means that we can't put our hands on them.

I Peter 5:8 — *"Be sober-minded; be watchful. Your adversary the devil prowls around like a roaring lion, seeking someone to devour."* (ESV)

I John 4:4 — *"Greater is He Who is in you than he who is in the world."* (KJV)

Matt. 18:19 — *"Again I say to you, that if two of you agree on earth about anything that they may ask, it shall be done for them by My Father who is in heaven."* (NASB)

Some of the most powerful prayers on the planet are generated by godly husbands and wives agreeing together and, through humble petitions and mighty declarations, releasing God's will to be done on earth as it is in heaven.

Finally, it's important to note that God gave the assignment to work together to Adam and Eve before the fall. He's never rescinded it. It was and still is part of His purpose for man and for marriage.

Here's a good question to ponder: If the garden of your marriage is less than the Eden God desires it to be, who's responsible?

The good news is that we can have the kind of marriage God intends, but we must approach it *intentionally*. Are you ready?

Some of the most powerful prayers on the planet are generated by godly husbands and wives agreeing together

26

CHAPTER 3

BE INTENTIONAL ABOUT...

COMMUNICATION

"... the root of all communication problems — can be understood as a deficit of love"[1] — Dr. Everett L. Worthington

THE VALUE OF COMMUNICATION

The ability to communicate well is probably the most important skill we bring to a relationship. As I (Dennis) counsel with couples, I find I can link almost every issue they struggle with to dysfunctional communication. For this reason, I'm convinced that marriages cannot grow and improve without intentionally developing communication skills.

Hurt feelings; financial misunderstandings; unsatisfied wants, needs, and desires; and the disappointment with sexual intimacy all have their roots in a lack of communication. In some cases, a couple's communication is so poor it does more damage than if they weren't communicating at all. Crucial to a healthy marriage is healthy communication.

Ask yourself a few hard questions if you dare:

Do you care more about whether your spouse understands you or you understand your spouse? Perhaps you're lacking love.

Are you more concerned about your spouse hearing you than about you hearing your spouse? This, too, may be an indication you have a deficit of love.

Love says, *I love you enough to make the effort necessary to understand you,*

Crucial to a healthy marriage is healthy communication.

27

whether you understand me or not. This is a leap of faith for some, but remember—we're not expecting everything to be fair. Instead, we're seeking to understand our spouses from a heart of love.

Let's look at some practical ways to communicate with love.

BE GENTLE

Dr. John Gottman, Director of the Relationship Research Institute, interviewed more than 3000 couples over a 35-year period. He discovered that couples who are gentle in their approach toward each other experience a higher level of satisfaction than those who are critical.[2]

This may seem like a no-brainer as you calmly read these words, but think about the last time you and your spouse had a heated discussion. It was very difficult to remember to be gentle in the heat of the moment, wasn't it? It takes practice and intentionality to conduct ourselves in a way contrary to how we feel.

Gottman discovered that when couples handled their conflicts with gentleness, each partner was willing to take responsibility for at least part of the problem. They recognized that most conflicts weren't just one person's fault.[3]

In contrast, when spouses did not approach the discussion with gentleness, instead of working toward a solution, they were more interested in pointing out the other person's flaws. They also expected to be appreciated for pointing out their partner's inadequacies.[4]

May I give you a heads up? Unless our spouses ask for our opinions or give permission to point out their mistakes, they will not appreciate our input. In most cases, our unsolicited advice will breed resentment. It's important to remember that it's not our responsibility to point out our spouses' flaws. Instead, we should accept responsibility and seek to address our own faults. It's also important to watch our tone of voice during a discussion. We should never sound like a parent speaking to a child. Being gentle with our spouses communicates respect.

Being gentle with our spouses communicates respect.

Softening our approach to a conversation is another effective way to communicate. Gottman reminds us to raise issues softly.[5] Discussions invariably end on the same note they began. If we start an argument by harshly attacking our partner, it will usually escalate, making the conflict much bigger than it needs to be.

Using foul or abusive language is another critical communication tactic. Instead, intentionally choosing good and helpful words enables us to encourage those who hear them. *"Get rid of all bitterness, rage, anger, harsh words, and slander, as well as all types of evil behavior. Instead, be kind to each other, tenderhearted, forgiving one another, just as God through Christ has forgiven you"* (Eph. 4: 29-32).

Being gentle or soft in our approach doesn't mean we're weak; it takes a lot of courage and maturity to communicate in this manner.

RESOLVE CONFLICT

It's unreasonable to expect that we'll never experience conflict in our marriages. Think for a moment about the reality of two people living together as husband and wife. The first challenge we experience is the differences between males and females—a subject broad enough to fill thousands of books.

The second challenge is that most couples come from vastly different backgrounds. My wife and I have joked for years about our different upbringings. She lived on the same street as the country club and thought everyone had a swimming pool. I was raised in the country and felt bad for people who didn't live in a mobile home like I did, because they had to leave their houses behind when they moved.

Each family of origin handled emotions, disappointments, and even tragedies differently. They handled finances, chores, and discipline in different ways, too. And then there were the differences in religion, politics, and morality.

In the heat of the moment, we tend to draw from our own family's method for handling issues, whether it was effective or not. Add each spouse's individual preferences, needs, desires, and wants, and we have real potential for conflict. From the start, there are already a lot of challenges in place when two people say *I do* in front of friends and family.

Because of these factors, conflict is inevitable, no matter how much we love each other. The good news is, if we find ourselves experiencing conflict, this usually means we care. If we didn't care about each other and our marriages, we wouldn't care enough to fight. The real issue is not whether we have conflict, but how we handle it that makes the difference.

As the title of this chapter indicates, it's important to be intentional about resolving conflict. Notice I didn't say be intentional about *avoiding* conflict. People who hate conflict will often attempt to avoid it altogether. To keep the peace, they allow others to disrespect, take advantage of, or shut them down completely.

The real issue is not whether we have conflict, but how we handle it that will make the difference.

But avoiding conflict doesn't make it go away. Since conflict and the resulting emotions have to go somewhere, if we don't deal with them in healthy ways, we wind up internalizing them. This shifts the conflict from the outside to the inside, causing emotional conflict that often resurfaces as depression, irritation, and/or low self-esteem.

It's obvious, then, that resolving conflict, not avoiding it, is the most effective strategy for a healthy marriage. Here are several effective ways to handle disagreements:

REACT VS. RESPOND

Remember, our parents, teachers, coaches, and friends were role models as we learned how to handle conflict. Whether these significant people reacted or responded set the example for whether we will react or respond. Let's look at the difference.

30

For most of us, reacting is our natural way to handle conflict. This approach comes from a programmed default mechanism. If our parents reacted in anger by throwing pots and pans, using foul language, or being physically abusive, this was our model. We may have hated the way they handled things, but as we encountered conflict, reacting in anger became our default method, too.

Communication

We got married, and the first big blowup erupted in a pot throwing, name calling, screaming match with no resolution. We reacted from our default mode, because we didn't know any other way to handle arguments or disagreements. It didn't work, but it was all we knew.

The good news is that we can reprogram our default mechanism. God created us with the ability to learn a different way to handle our lives. We're not stuck with what we learned growing up. One of the frequent lies I hear from people is, "Well, that's just the way I am." This may be how we are today, but we don't have to stay this way. We can change the way we think, act, and feel.

Reacting is a natural instinct, and one we share with the animal world. But while animals rely primarily on instinct to survive, humans have the added ability to reason and respond, not just react.

RESPOND

While reacting is a response based on instinct and rooted in the past, responding involves thinking through a situation before acting. It allows thought rather than emotion to dictate what we do. It requires that we intentionally choose not to act on instinct or emotion, but, instead, to think ahead to the possible consequences of our actions.

As I help people learn to respond versus react, I encourage them to do this very simple exercise: The next time you find yourself in the middle of an argument, intentionally stop and take a deep breath (yes, the old adage about counting to ten does help). Give yourself a moment to collect your thoughts. (Keep in mind, this is a skill you can develop.) During this moment, ask yourself the following question:

What do I hope to accomplish with what I intend to say?

Your answer will determine whether you want to use your words to help clarify a situation or to harm your spouse.

Here's a helpful exercise to use when we anticipate an argument—when we're late getting home, for example. Before we enter the situation, take time to anticipate our spouse's emotions and then develop a response. Lest you think I'm encouraging you to make up an excuse before you get home, I'm suggesting no such thing. Our goal is to determine what we're going to say ("Honey, I'm sorry I'm late."), instead of entering into a shouting match because we're trying to win an argument rather than resolve it.

In the next two chapters, we'll look at harmful relationship reactions and consider how substituting helpful relationship responses can lead to a healthier, happier marriage environment.

What do I hope to accomplish with what I intend to say?

CHAPTER 4

BE INTENTIONAL ABOUT ...

HARMFUL
RELATIONSHIP
REACTIONS

As we realized in the previous chapter, reacting instead of responding can be extremely destructive to our communication, and, ultimately, our marriages. Let's look at several harmful reaction responses, the motivation behind them, and their potential effects on our relationships.

Threats (divorce, separation, etc.).

At all cost, avoid threats. This is the same advice I give parents about threatening their children. A threat is only as good as the follow through, and threats are meant to intimidate and control. Before we make a threat, we must ask ourselves, *Is this what I'm really trying to do? Am I hoping to control or intimidate my mate?* If so, this is not a healthy way to live in relationship.

Threats can be even more damaging in a marriage than in a parent/child relationship. Every time we use a threat (*If you come home late again, I'll leave you*), we plant fear in our spouse's minds. Over time, this continual threatening causes wounds and scars that are difficult to recover from.

In our marriage seminars, we strongly advise that the word *divorce* is also a no-no. No matter how difficult our marriages are, it's important to remember and declare, "Divorce is not an option."

No matter how difficult our marriages are, it's important to remember and declare, "Divorce is not an option."

This may seem very narrow, but taking this option off the table is often a very helpful step on the path toward healing.

COMEBACKS

Comebacks occur when we answer a complaint with a complaint of our own. Our spouse accuses, "You forgot to close the cap on the toothpaste again," and we come back with, "Well, you forget to lock the door." What we're really saying with a comeback is, *I'm not willing to take responsibility for what you pointed out, so I'm going to point out something you didn't do.* You know, like when we were in third grade.

The problem is, we're not in third grade anymore. We're adults. When our spouses point out things that bother them, we can and should take responsibility. "You're right honey (taking responsibility) I'll make sure I close the toothpaste cap from now on."

HAND GRENADES

In one counseling session, I (Dennis) sat and listened while a husband and wife tossed barbs back and forth at each other. At one point, I called a truce and said, "The picture I see is two people, each barricaded behind a wall of hurt, tossing grenades at each other over the walls." One of the most common questions I ask in a situation like this is, "What are you hoping to accomplish with your grenades?"

When we lob verbal grenades at each other, we're usually hoping to hurt the other person because they've hurt us, but this doesn't resolve the conflict or heal the relationship. In most cases, it just causes more damage, which leads to more hurt.

We must intentionally avoid these relationship hand grenades:

Exaggerations

Let's be honest. We've all done it. In the heat of the moment, we pull facts and figures out of the air and state them as truth. "I've told you a million times to pick up your socks!" Come on, really? It might feel like a million times, but that's an exaggeration.

You never … and You always …

"You *never* tell me when you're going to come home late." Never? That's an eternal word. Again, it might feel like our spouses never do something, but that's an exaggeration. *Never* and *always* are big eternal words. Is it true that your spouse *never* comes home on time? Is it true that your *spouse always* forgets to call?

If our goal is to resolve conflict, starting a sentence with *you never* or *you always* doesn't usually cause the conversation to end well. These words send us down a negative road. Rather than using these eternal phrases, we can be very specific when communicating what's troubling us. "I was really upset when you came home late." This is neither an exaggeration nor an accusation. It states the facts and expresses how we feel.

Before speaking, we can ask ourselves if *never* or *always* is accurate. Perhaps softer and more accurate words such as, *I feel like you never … or It seems like you always …* might be better choices.

Here are some other examples:

"I've told you *many* times to pick up your socks"

"You *frequently* don't let me know that you're going to be late"

Keep in mind that exaggerations have a way of discrediting what we say. The person on the other end of our exaggeration is offended that we've distorted the truth and won't take seriously what we're trying to communicate. It's pointless to paint the picture in a ridiculous way hoping our spouses will be embarrassed enough to make a change. Many times when we use exaggerations, we follow up by saying, "I was just trying to make a point"

My advice—just make the point. Describe how we feel rather than exaggerate.

Harmful Relationship Reactions

Keep in mind that exaggerations have a way of discrediting what we say.

Another futile communication tactic is accusations. We accuse the other person without having any facts. We may be working from a history with this person, but in the moment, we're just guessing. We say, "You'd rather spend your time at the office than be home with me."

We usually accuse from a place of hurt. We feel cheated, abandoned, or ignored in some way. We say, "I bet you didn't even think about stopping at the store."

Accusations will immediately put our spouses in a defensive posture. Once they're in a defensive posture, they'll defend themselves at any cost. Because of this, accusations have the power to cause much hurt and accomplish very little.

Rather than making an accusation, it's often helpful to ask questions or make a request.

"I feel like you'd rather spend time at the office instead of here with me."

"Next time, would you please stop at the store?"

Keep in mind that an accusation is an aggressive tactic that elevates the issue rather than resolves it.

Intimidation

Intimidation can take many forms. Verbal, physical, and emotional intimidations are the most common.

Physical intimidation can range from simply towering over someone to overpowering a person with brute force to cause physical harm.

What are some examples of physical intimidation? Suppose the discussion heats up. One person stands while the other remains seated. She might even lean over the table or desk to demonstrate strength or leverage and raise her voice.

Or perhaps one spouse becomes so frustrated with the course

of the argument that he resorts to grabbing his wife around the throat, punching her in the face, or tossing her against a wall. This sounds very dramatic, but it's a reality in many homes.

PLEASE NOTE: If you find yourself in a potentially harmful situation, you have a right to protect yourself. Remove yourself from the situation until you can get help.

Verbal intimidation is another form of abuse. Name-calling, foul language, or angry shouting are all attempts to intimidate our spouses. We can't allow ourselves to be drawn into a battle like this; it seldom ends well.

Emotional intimidation is a form of manipulation. Crying, pouting, hysterics, and even head games are attempts to control or intimidate. Twisting what the other person says, being sarcastic, or belittling are other tools of the emotional intimidator.

Assumptions

Unless we're mind readers (and if we really can read minds, let's hit the road with a circus), we can only assume we know what our spouses are thinking. Granted, based on history or pattern with our spouses, we can make a good guess, but assuming we know sets us up for a nasty fight.

Example: We observe our spouse rolling her eyes when we make a statement. Our first response is "I see you rolling your eyes. I know what that means." The question is: Do you really?

In a recent counseling session, a husband was sharing that his wife had not communicated how she felt. He suddenly stopped speaking and commented, "I see you shaking your head." Then he launched into the black hole of assuming she was disagreeing with him.

When I called a quick timeout, I asked his wife what she meant by shaking her head. She said, "I was actually agreeing with him that I had not communicated how I felt." She was shaking her head *no*, while actually agreeing with him.

In a seminar I conducted on body language, I gave examples of how we unconsciously communicate using our hands and feet. I used the example of crossed arms. Most of the time, when we want to communicate that we're not open to what someone is saying we consciously or unconsciously cross our arms.

One man in the group raised his hand and said, "Now I understand." He shared that his wife often walks into a room and notices his folded arms. Picking up on his defensive posture, she asks, "What are you mad about?"

"And I always say, 'Nothing.'" He explained he wasn't mad about anything; he just doesn't know what to do with his arms while sitting, so he crosses them.

So how do we keep from assuming we know what our spouses are thinking?

We check it out.

What does this look like? Let's replay one of the previous examples. When the husband observed his wife shaking her head while he was speaking, he could pause for a moment, look her in the eyes, and ask, "I noticed you shaking your head. What do you mean by that?" This does two things:

It lets your spouse know you're observant.

It prevents you from assuming.

Sarcasm

Ah yes … sarcasm. It's an old friend to some. When I was in junior high school, I was a tall, skinny kid who was a natural target for bullies. I quickly realized that although I didn't stand a chance in a physical battle, I could use my wit to embarrass a bully in front of his friends. Since I had a knack for humor, adding sarcasm was a natural fit. The challenge with sarcasm, though, is that it can become our default setting when we encounter conflicts.

Sarcasm is a passive/aggressive way to address something that bothers us. For example, our spouse has a habit of leaving late for

Sarcasm is a passive/aggressive way to address something that bothers us.

38

appointments. As she makes her way to the car, we say, "Well, I guess we don't have to worry about getting there too early, do we?"

Here's a question to consider: If our intent is to address the issue of lateness, how does this help? Do we really believe a sarcastic remark will cause our spouse to admit her weakness, decide to change her habit, or apologize for causing us to be late?

Here's another question: Has this method worked in the past?

Even though it hasn't, we continue to use sarcasm as a way to vent our frustrations.. What if there was a way to address the situation that really works?

Good news! You're reading the right book. Try this next time: Your spouse is habitually late leaving the house, which causes you to be late because you ride together. Plan to talk to your spouse at a time when you're not late, frustrated, or in public. Without being sarcastic, share how frustrated you feel when you're late. Suggest a solution that would be helpful to both of you. "When we are late leaving, I feel very frustrated. I'd like to leave on time in the future. Are you willing to do that?" Then take it one step further and ask, "Is there anything that I can do to help us leave on time?"

We've spent considerable time talking about harmful relationship reactions. Now that we understand their destructive nature, let's talk about an alternative to reacting—responding.

CHAPTER 5

BE INTENTIONAL ABOUT . . .

POWERFUL RELATIONSHIP RESPONSES

Now that we've thoroughly examined the destructive arsenal of emotional reactions, let's examine five powerful relationship responses. We can substitute these responses for reactions as we seek to build effective communication in our marriages. These responses include extending forgiveness, communicating worth, paying compliments, extending respect, and expressing affirmation.

EXTEND FORGIVENESS

Forgiveness is a gift.

We might say, "He hurt me. Why would I want to give him a gift?"

Forgiveness is one of the ways to release ourselves from the past.

Forgiveness is primarily a gift we give ourselves. As long as we harbor unforgiveness, we remain connected to the hurt and to the one who hurt us. As long as we choose not to forgive, by default we also choose to maintain a connection to the hurtful event, relationship, and in some cases, the person who hurt us.

Give yourself a gift—extend forgiveness. Forgiveness is one of the ways to release ourselves from the past.

It's important to remember that forgiveness is not forgetting.

We may never forget the hurt that has caused us pain.

When I (Dennis) work with those who have been the victims of sexual abuse, for example, it's painfully clear how impossible it is for them to forget what happened. Although we still may remember the painful event, choosing to forgive allows us to intentionally re-frame the way we see it. In simple terms, when we remember the hurt, we also remember that we have decided to forgive. This takes the sting of remembering and turns it into the freedom of forgiving.

Forgiveness is a choice.

Just like forgiveness is not forgetting, choosing to forgive is not condoning the other person's actions. Forgiveness is not giving in, or saying it doesn't matter. Instead, it's choosing to release the urge for revenge. When we've been hurt, our natural reaction is to hurt or want to see the other person hurt. Sometimes the urge for revenge is so strong, we even put ourselves at risk to see the other person suffer.

We've all heard this phrase relating to resentment, but I'll use literary license here and insert the word *unforgiveness*. *Unforgiveness is like drinking poison hoping the other person dies.* In most cases, the hurt and unforgiveness we hold onto only affects us. The other person has already moved on or doesn't even realize what their actions produced.

Anytime we wrestle with forgiving someone, we should remember a time when we desperately needed forgiveness.

One of the greatest motivations we can bring to this issue of forgiveness is the forgiveness we've personally experienced because of Christ's work on the cross. Because God has forgiven us, so we must also forgive others.

If someone displayed our lives on a movie screen or spreadsheet, we'd quickly see how many offenses for which God has forgiven us. We owe a great debt of gratitude. One way to express our thankfulness to God for His forgiveness is to forgive others.

Anytime we wrestle with forgiving someone, we should remember a time when we desperately needed forgiveness. Each of us, at some time in our lives, has received mercy in the form of forgiveness. Mercy can be defined simply as *not being punished as we deserve.*

The Word reminds us in Matthew 7:2, *"For you will be treated as you treat others. The standard you use in judging is the standard by which you will be judged."* If we desire mercy, then we must be willing to extend this same grace in the form of forgiveness.

Jesus indicated that forgiveness should have no limits. In Matthew 18, Peter asked Jesus how many times he should forgive someone who sinned against him. Jesus replied, *"Seven times seventy."* Forgiveness, then, becomes a lifestyle, not just a treat we extend on special occasions. It's about choosing how we handle a past hurt rather than passively allowing the hurt to continue to affect us. When we choose to forgive, we take charge of the situation.

Forgiveness is about regaining control in our lives. We move from being a victim to a victor. Forgiveness is a tool we employ to keep our own spirits clean and prevent bitterness from growing.

"Forgiving is the only way to heal the wounds of a past we cannot change and cannot forget," says James Beck in his book, *Jesus & Personality Theory: Exploring the Five-Factor Model.* Harboring unforgiveness ties us to the offense or hurt and delays the healing process.

The essence of forgiveness is letting go of the need for revenge and further restitution The never-ending quest for revenge drags us into the deep, dark hole of spite and vengeance. It's true that the best revenge is to be the best we can be in our own lives. Extending forgiveness and moving on is a positive response to a negative situation.

Forgiveness is a choice we make and not based on a guarantee of never being hurt again. Many times what we're looking for in an apology is a guarantee. Unfortunately, in human relationships, there are no guarantees. Keep in mind, however, that a trained counselor can help you set healthy boundaries in your relationship. These boundaries are not guarantees, but they can help you create a safety buffer for yourself and your emotions.

Forgiveness is about regaining control in our lives.

Forgiveness is a choice we make and not based on a guarantee of never being hurt again.

COMMUNICATE WORTH

I have two sets of golf clubs. One is an old set that someone gave me years ago. It was a great first set for a hacker like me. Recently, someone gave me a nicer set of clubs. I really enjoy taking this set out for 18 holes on a sunny day, especially since my precious wife bought me a new driver for my birthday.

Powerful Relationship Responses

If you were to ask me if you could borrow my old set of clubs, I wouldn't hesitate. "Sure," I'd say "go have a great time." Why would I be so quick to lend this set of clubs? Because even though they carry some measure of worth, they're not as valuable to me as my newer set.

If you asked to borrow my new set, however, I'd have to know you really well, and you might have to fill out an application and leave a deposit (just kidding ... but not much). I'd want to be sure you'd take care of them. Why? Because they are worth more to me, and I value them.

Here's a question to consider: How much do you value your spouse?

We'd all probably say we consider our spouses important, worthwhile, and a priority, but do our actions back up our words?

When the boss offers a last-minute invitation to attend a business social after work, do we consider our spouses? Do we ask our boss to give us a minute to check with her before we answer, or do we immediately say *yes* and justify it later by saying, "But the boss asked me."

Communicating worth involves being kind, courteous, gentle, thoughtful, and honoring.

When we walk into the room, do we grab the remote and change the channel without considering what our spouses might be watching? When we're hanging out with friends, do we make jokes about our spouses, at their expense? Do we accept the kind things they do on our behalves as something they owe us, or do we respond with thankfulness and gratitude?

"Wherever your treasure is, there the desires of your heart will also be" (Matthew 6:21 NLT).

Communicating worth involves being kind, courteous, gentle, thoughtful, and honoring. Little attitudes like these make a difference in a relationship. Communicating worth also includes extending courtesies, like saying *please* and *thank you* to each other.

"Thank you for folding the clothes."

"Would you please take out the trash?"

"I appreciate you making dinner."

Does this sound silly? Remember, it's the little things that make a difference. These small acts communicate worth. When we're intentionally grateful, appreciative, honoring, thoughtful, and courteous; we demonstrate that we value our spouses. Instead of accepting the kind things they do on our behalf as if they are something they owe us, acknowledging them with a grateful heart builds an atmosphere of mutual appreciation.

PAY COMPLIMENTS AND EXTEND RESPECT

We're often more polite to strangers than to our spouses. When we meet someone for the first time, we're typically very congenial and polite. We treat a new employee at work with kindness and courtesy. When we're around the ones we love and share life with, however, it's often a different story. We feel we have the right to act disrespectfully to each other. Rather than cultivating an environment of kindness and courtesy, we foster a climate of sharp speech, rude interaction, and self-entitlement.

We're often more polite to strangers than to our spouses.

Our children, all grown now, sometimes giggle and make fun of us when they hear us thank each other during the course of the day or show appreciation for something one of us has done for the other.

"Honey, thank you for folding the clothes."

"Sweetheart, I appreciate you making dinner tonight."

We know, though, that they appreciate the courtesy we demonstrate toward each other and pray to one day have spouses who

44

do the same. As a couple that has been to Hell and back over the course of our 30-year marriage, we understand the value of showing respect, appreciation, courtesy, and kindness. We understand that courtesy equals respect.

On a normal day, it sounds like this: "Would you please replace the light bulb in the bathroom?" or, "We've been invited to dinner on Friday night. Do you have any other plans? Would you like to go?"

Keep in mind that our tone of voice can also communicate these same statements sarcastically. As we'll learn in a subsequent chapter, this can be very destructive. We must communicate courtesy, kindness, appreciation, and gratitude with sincerity.

PRACTICE AFFIRMATION

Earlier we discovered how accusations are one of the communication hand grenades we want to avoid. A healthy alternative to accusations is affirmation. Because of our default settings, it's easy to accuse, but more challenging to affirm. We're quick to try to catch each other doing something wrong, instead of eagerly looking for what the other is doing right.

We want to create a safe and positive environment. If the climate in our homes is full of suspicion and accusations, this will lead to a perpetually negative environment. If our relationships are characterized by affirmation, encouragement, and appreciation, we'll create a positive atmosphere that sustains and grows our relationships.

Keep in mind that when we communicate, we demonstrate that we care. Communication, however, is much more than what we say. Our body language, emotion, tone, and how we phrase things are all part of getting our message across. When we experience a communication conflict, it's often caused by *how* we say something, not *what* we say. Couples in an intentional marriage carefully consider how they communicate.

45

CHAPTER 6

BE INTENTIONAL ABOUT...

TAKING CARE
OF OURSELVES

As a women's healthcare provider, one of the saddest things I (Susan) see is what happens when a husband or wife stops caring for his or her body. While it used to be a priority to eat right, exercise, and watch their weight, it is no longer. They let themselves go, and the results are devastating.

I'll never forget one patient weeping in anguish and anger over her husband's choice not to treat his diabetes and hypertension with prescribed medication and lifestyle changes. His neglect of his body and health had led to impotence, which affected not only him, but her also. "I'm only 47," she said, "and I don't get to have sex with my husband anymore, because he's not taking care of himself. I've lost an important part of my life, and I miss it!"

I wish I could say this is an isolated occurrence, but it's not.

Many think, because they've already caught their spouses, that they no longer need to spend the time and effort to maintain their attractiveness. They think their marital vows should be enough to keep their spouses committed.

Let me respond to this with a question. Are you ok with the possibility that your spouse stays in your marriage with you solely because he or she made a vow to do so? What if they knew how things would become with you, and given the opportunity (ok, just roll with this hypothetical situation for a moment) to have a do over, they wouldn't make the same choice again? Yep, that's a sad, sad way to end up … but it doesn't have to be this way.

Let me respond to this with a few questions: Are you satisfied that the only reason your spouse stays married to you is because of the vow he/she made? What if he/she had been able to look into the future to where you are now? Would he/she make the same commitment again?

Being *intentional* is not just a principle that applies to our marriages; it can and should affect every area of our lives, including our physical bodies.

Paul clearly communicates, in I Cor. 6:19 that it matters to God how we care for our bodies. *"Or do you not know that your body is the temple of the Holy Spirit Who is in you, whom you have from God, and you are not your own?"* (NKJV) God is very interested in how we care for our bodies, because they house His Spirit. He chooses to place Himself, as the Holy Spirit, inside our bodies, and we become His temple. Not only that, we now belong to Him; we are not our own anymore.

God is very interested in how we care for our bodies, because they house His Spirit.

In this passage, we see that the word body is the Greek word *soma*, which speaks of the physical, fleshly body of men or animals. It originates from the word *sozo*, which means "to save, keep safe, to rescue from danger and destruction." This word, *sozo*, refers to the salvation Jesus came to bring. Matthew 18:11 illustrates this, "For the Son of Man has come to save that which was lost." This saving, however, doesn't just refer to being saved from our sins. It also extends to our physical bodies in the form of healing and restoration.

Paul further illustrates this connection between our body and the Holy Spirit in Romans 8:11, which states, *"The Spirit of God, who raised Jesus from the dead, lives in you. And just as God raised Christ Jesus from the dead, he will give life to your mortal bodies by this same Spirit living within you."* (NLT) The word *body* in this passage is the word *soma*—our fleshly body. The word *life* is the Greek word *zōopoieō* and includes in its definition, "to cause to live, make alive, give life; to give increase of life: thus of physical life." Therefore, we can conclude that the presence of the Spirit that raised Jesus from the dead living inside our physical bodies has the potential to enhance the quality of life of our bodies. Indeed, how could it not?

God the Holy Spirit chooses to make our *soma* (physical, fleshly body) His temple (*naos*). This word, *naos*, speaks of the Holy place—the Holy of Holies portion of the temple. The root word is *naio*, which means "to dwell." Let's put it all together: God comes inside, makes us His own (We no longer belong to ourselves, because we've been "bought with a price" according to I Corinthians 6:20), takes up residence, brings life, and restores and heals every part of us. In other words, being His temple allows Him to save (*sozo*) us to the uttermost! (Hebrews 7:25). What a great place to say, "Hallelujah!"

Being conscious of the fact that we are now His, the next logical question is, "What is our responsibility?" Paul, the apostle, answers this question in Romans 12: 1, "*I beseech you therefore, brethren, by the mercies of God, that ye present your bodies a living sacrifice, holy, acceptable unto God, [which is] your reasonable service*" (NKJV). In order to fully understand the magnitude of this verse, we need to examine some key words in their original Greek.

The word present (*paristemi*) means, "To place beside or near (a person or thing at one's disposal); to stand ready to help." In other words, my physical body (*soma*), which is now the temple (*naos*) of His Holy Spirit, is to be given to Jesus, and is now available, at His disposal, to be used to help others.

Remembering that *soma* is derived from *sozo*, which speaks of salvation, I can conclude that I'm now able to be an extension of Him to others who need His *sozo* (salvation). Therefore, in His sovereign, magnificent plan, my physical body, inhabited by His Spirit, becomes a tool that's available to bring the Good News of salvation to the lost. This is evangelism at its absolute best.

The word living (*zao*) is defined as "to live, breathe, be among the living; (metaphor) to be in full vigour; to enjoy real life; active; to be fresh, strong, powerful." By using this word, Paul qualifies the kind of body (*soma*) we are to present to the Lord—a body that's alive, full of vigor (energetic), active, strong, powerful, and one that enjoys real life. This person isn't just sitting around, passively existing. He/she is active and intentional about the way they care for their bodies, and it's evident in the daily choices they make concerning their health.

Because of their intentional choices, they enjoy the abundant life Jesus speaks of in John 10:10. He states that His purpose for coming is "that they may have life (*zoe*), and have it abundantly." The word for life, *zoe*, in this passage comes from the word *zao* that Paul uses in Romans 12:1.

Finally, Paul says that this offering of a body (*soma*) that's living (*zao*) is a reasonable act of service to the Lord. The Greek word used here is *logikos*, and it speaks of that "pertaining to speech, speaking, reason, or logic." It originates from the word *logos*, which is one of the Greek words that also refers to the Word of God. It involves "a word, uttered by a living voice, embodying a conception or idea; the mental faculty of thinking, meditating, reasoning, and calculating." We can derive from this description that thoughtful planning is necessary in order to present bodies that are living and useful to God.

Thoughtful planning is necessary in order to present bodies that are living and useful to God.

To think that being a healthy person, with all that the word *zao* embodies, is something that just happens is the equivalent of believing that beautiful landscaping or spectacular buildings magically appear without any planning or effort. As a healthcare provider, however, I've observed choices my patients have made concerning their bodies using this form of erroneous logic.

Now that we've established the spiritual reasons for taking care of our bodies, let's examine one very important relational reason—our responsibility to our spouses.

Paul addresses God's perspective on this in I Corinthians 7:4: "*The wife does not have authority over her own body, but the husband does; and likewise also the husband does not have authority over his own body, but the wife does.*" (NASB)

49

The NIV states this responsibility even more bluntly: *"The wife's body does not belong to her alone, but also to her husband. In the same way, the husband's body does not belong to him alone, but also to his wife."*

According to God's plan, when we marry, we surrender the right to do with our bodies whatever we want. We're now responsible to consider our spouses in all our decisions, especially regarding choices that affect our health. Not only do the choices we make affect us, they also, eventually, affect our spouses. When we say our vows, we promise to care for our spouses for life. We can't do this if we are careless or negligent with our health.

Not only do the choices we make affect us, they'll also, eventually, affect our spouses.

It's important to note then, that caring for our bodies is not only an act of service and worship to God, it's also a benefit and service to our mates. Now let's get practical.

FIVE INTENTIONAL HEALTH HABITS

PRACTICE HEART HEALTH.

Heart disease is the number one killer of American men and women. One of the most important components of heart health involves our blood pressure. It's important to check our numbers regularly, especially if we have a family history of hypertension.

Normal blood pressure is 120/80 or lower. Prehypertension is 120-139/80-89. It's crucial to reduce the amount of sodium in our diets if we struggle with high blood pressure. Of all the elements in our bodies, sodium has the greatest impact on blood pressure.

While this seems like a simple step, it's one of many we can take to positively affect our heart health. Talking with our health care providers about other ways, including medication and/or lifestyle changes, can help us partner with him/her and address this significant issue.

The desirable target for one's total cholesterol level is less than 200.

People are often confused about the difference between "bad cholesterol" (LDL) and "good cholesterol" (HDL). Here's an easy way to remember it: Think of the *L*, in LDL (Low-density lipoprotein), as *L*ousy and the *H* in HDL (High-density lipoprotein) as *H*appy.

A level of less than 100 is considered optimal for LDL. We want to keep this cholesterol component in the desirable range because of its involvement in heart disease. Health care providers will frequently prescribe cholesterol medication if LDL levels are too high..

The ideal range for your HDL level is varies for men and women. The number to strive for in men is greater than 50 mg/dL. For women, greater than 40 mg/dL is the goal. For this particular cholesterol, the higher the number, the better it is for your heart. Experts also consider a higher number a negative risk factor. If it's elevated, it can actually negate some of the risk for heart disease. Exercising regularly in a manner that raises our heart rate and makes us sweat is a natural way to raise this number.

A third piece in the cholesterol puzzle is the triglyceride element. Triglycerides are the chemical forms in which most fats exist in food as well as in the body. These come from converted energy sources like carbohydrates. A level of less than 150 is the desirable goal.

For more comprehensive information on how to prevent heart disease, visit the American Heart Association website (http://www.heart.org/HEARTORG/).

MAINTAIN A HEALTHY WEIGHT.

While we're being intentional about bodies, it's crucial to maintain a healthy weight. BMI (Body Mass Index) is the lens we use to assess weight in determining fitness. BMI is a calculation involving the ratio of height and weight. (For more information on calculating

Taking Care of Ourselves

your BMI, visit the American Heart Association website at http://www.heart.org). Here's a breakdown of the numbers:

< 25 = *healthy weight*
$25-29$ = *overweight*
> 29 = *obesity*

To achieve and maintain a healthy weight, it's important to practice healthy eating choices and exercise regularly. Moderation and portion size are the keys to healthy eating, and exercise doesn't have to be structured or costly. Look for ways to incorporate exercise and fitness activities into your daily routine. Be creative about finding opportunities to exercise together. Walking is a simple, inexpensive exercise that can shrink your waistline and grow your relationship. So is lovemaking.

Investing in a pedometer is one way to become more conscious of the need to move our bodies. A reasonable goal of 10,000 steps (approximately 5 miles) each day is very doable. Remember, this count includes the total accumulation of walking during the entire day—the steps you take at work, while running errands, and during your walk as a couple. And don't discredit the exercise technology available through the Wii™ systems. Fitness really can be fun. And if you think you simply don't have a way to exercise, remember the old saying, *we find a way to do what we really want to do.*

Partnering together in our quest for a healthier lifestyle is essential for unity and success. "Adam Shafran, DC, an exercise physiologist and chiropractor who also hosts *Dr. Fitness and the Fat Guy*, an Internet radio show focusing on weight loss, says people fail not necessarily because they're following a bad weight loss plan, but because they lack a good support system. 'It can be the deciding factor that makes a diet work -- or not work,' says Shafran." [2]

A final benefit to partnering together in health is that it helps promote intimacy. Unfortunately, we often limit intimacy to the context of the bedroom, and as married couples, this isn't a big stretch. Intimacy, in its broadest form, however, involves not only

52

the physical act of sexual relations, but more importantly, the emotional warmth and closeness that bonds a couple together for life. This bonding can and should be the foundation for satisfying sexual relations.

SCHEDULE ANNUAL PHYSICALS.

Another way we can be good stewards of our physical bodies is by having an annual physical that includes appropriate labs and studies. The list of lab work that should be collected and evaluated can be extensive and is something you and your healthcare provider should discuss. Routine labs might include a complete metabolic panel that evaluates some of the body's electrolytes, kidney, and liver function, as well as a lipid panel to evaluate cholesterol levels.

I also suggest checking several other levels essential to overall physical and mental well-being. Ask your healthcare professional about including thyroid hormone labs and Vitamin D levels. While the thyroid gland doesn't control any major system of the body, it does affect all of them. Elevated or decreased thyroid levels can also affect our moods. Vitamin D levels should be assessed by a blood test known as a Vitamin D 25-Hydroxy. While scientists are still studying the scope of Vitamin D's usefulness to our bodies, the latest research shows its importance to many organs. It's theorized that insufficient amounts may even be linked to some disease processes.

If you're a middle-aged man, and you or your spouse notice changes in your mood, stamina, and sexual ability, it might be wise to have your testosterone level evaluated. Although easily assessed with a simple blood test, this test is not one health care professionals routinely order unless a patient mentions these symptoms.

A deficiency in this very important hormone can create a lot of physical, mental, and emotional stress for a couple. The good news is that for many who are suffering with a diminished testosterone level, there is hormone replacement therapy (HRT) available. It's not just for women anymore. Your healthcare provider can discuss the risks and benefits of this treatment and determine if you're a candidate.

MANAGE STRESS.

Our focus thus far has been on how to intentionally care for our bodies. We can't however, overlook the importance carrying for our emotional health. In Jude 1:20, we read God's prescription for stress management: *"But you, beloved, building yourselves up on your most holy faith, praying in the Holy Spirit."* There isn't time or space to extol the virtues of praying in the Spirit, but this is God's way of "building us up." And someone who is built up is better able to withstand the erosive effects of daily stress. Praying in the Spirit should be as much a part of our daily activities as exercising and brushing our teeth.

When we choose to live wisely and be good stewards of our bodies, we have the power of heaven available to assist us.

Finally, while I firmly believe in God's power to heal and redeem us from the curse of genetic predispositions, I also believe we have a responsibility to partner with Him in making healthy choices. Realizing we have more than ourselves to consider (friends, family, and especially our spouses) should greatly impact the choices we make over the course of our lives. When we choose to live wisely and be good stewards of our bodies, we have the power of heaven available to assist us. God won't, however, do for us what we can do for ourselves.

Remember our marriages and our bodies are like gardens. How well are we cultivating and keeping them?

CHAPTER 7

BE INTENTIONAL ABOUT...

A HEALTHY RELATIONSHIP

Great marriages doesn't just happen. Sometimes we get lazy and forget that healthy relationships take effort, hard work, and intentionality. In this chapter, we'll explore the necessary components of a healthy marriage. Some will come naturally, others will require determination, but all will require us to be intentional.

TRUST

What takes years to acquire, but can be lost in a moment? Trust.

Because trust is easily lost and difficult to regain, we must guard it vigilantly. It's the valuable glue that holds a relationship together. Without trust, each partner must maintain a continually guarded state for fear the other may prove untrustworthy. And while we can't earn trust, we can build it. There are no shortcuts.

Many couples come to me (Dennis) for counseling and express why they are unable to trust each other. Affairs, lies, gambling debts, porn ... the list goes on and on.

One of the statements I often hear is, "He/she doesn't trust me anymore." This is usually followed by, "How can I get him/her to trust me again?" It's often difficult for the one who has broken trust to understand why it's so hard for the other to trust again. After all, they've apologized and promised never to lie, cheat, or deceive, again. Can't we all just forgive and forget, and move on?

Unfortunately, it's not that easy.

For the one who's experienced a broken trust, it's a significant challenge to be able to trust again. What the offended spouse would like is a guarantee that the offense will never be repeated. Since this isn't realistic, they wonder what to do.

What can we do to restore trust?

We can apply the Gottman 5:1 Ratio. John Gottman, a clinical psychologist renowned for his work on marital stability and divorce prediction and founder of the Gottman Institute, discovered that for happy couples, there were five positive interactions for every negative one. If we're attempting to rebuild trust, we can employ this ratio to mean that it takes five times the effort to rebuild trust once it's broken.[1]

A key to restoring trust between spouses is becoming a trustworthy person. This begins by being a man/woman of our word. If we say we're going to do something, we do it. It's not rocket science; it's actually very simple. If we declare that we're *never* going to do something, we must be very intentional about never doing it again.

Over time, and it will take time, we become a more trustworthy person. As we start to become someone other people trust, we'll also begin rebuilding trust with our spouses.

The picture that I've often used describes the difference between building a poorly designed shack on your property, versus constructing a custom built home. It doesn't take an expert to recognize the difference between a structure than can be trusted and one that cannot.

As we rebuild trust with our spouses, it's important to approach it intentially. As we become more trustworthy, our spouses will begin to see the difference and will start to trust us again.

If I tell my wife that I won't ever do something again, you can be sure she'll be watching to see if I keep my word. If my wife tells me that she'll do something, of course I'll be watching to see if she keeps her word.

Obviously, it's important that we move beyond trying to catch each other being dishonest. If you begin to show ourselves as trustworthy, however, our spouses' fears will gradually decrease.

It is imperative that both spouses agree upon what is necessary to rebuild the trust between them. The offended spouse should be free to express what he/she feels it will take for him/her to regain trust. This is not a blank check to keep the offender eternally indebted, nor does it give the offended spouse the right to lord over the other for the rest of their relationship. The goal is not to police the offender, but to restore trust in the relationship. A professional counselor can help develop a strategy to bring healing to the relationship and restore trust.

An overused adage is "Talk is cheap." For good measure, here's another one: "Actions speak louder than words." It's important to remember that it takes time, patience, and consistency to rebuild trust. The first step is to be intentional about becoming a trust-worthy person. It's hard work, but it's worth it.

GENEROSITY

A study conducted by the University of Virginia National Marriage Project discovered that generosity (defined here as small acts of kindness, regular displays of affection and respect, and a willing-ness to forgive one's spouse their faults and failings) was positively associated with marital satisfaction and negatively associated with marital conflict and perceived divorce likelihood.[2]

This sounds like a no brainer, but how many of us routinely practice generosity in our relationships? Not just monetary gener-osity, but also relational generosity? Here are a few practical ways to be generous in our relationships:

BE GENEROUS WITH GRACE.

Remember that grace is giving what the other person doesn't de-

Remember that grace is giving what the other person doesn't deserve.

serve. If our spouses come home with sour attitudes, our natural reaction is to get offended and respond in kind. If we're generous with grace, however, we choose to act against our natural inclinations and respond instead in a compassionate and understanding way. We give them what they don't deserve—a gracious response—not with a haughty spirit, with love.

BE GENEROUS BY LISTENING.

Listening generously means being in the moment with your spouse.

How many of us spend as much time thinking of what to say as we do intentionally listening to the other person? My mom used to say, "God gave you two ears and only one mouth, so listen more than you talk." It's still good advice.

Listening generously means being in the moment with your spouse. Not thinking about all of the other things we need to do, or what we're missing on TV, or how hungry we are. We are in the zone and really hearing what our spouses are saying. A tool that helps me listen generously is to repeat back what my wife says occasionally during the conversation. This helps me communicate that I've really heard what she said.

BE GENEROUS WITH FORGIVENESS.

Forgiveness becomes a love gift we give each other.

We talked extensively about forgiveness in Chapter 5, but it's important enough to repeat. Forgiveness is a gift, both for the person offended and for the one who offended.

We should be generous with the benefit of the doubt and not quick to be suspicious or get offended. With maturity comes the ability not to take offence at everything. As we grow deeper in our love and respect for each other, forgiveness becomes a love gift we give each other.

58

Again, we've mentioned this in another section, but we can never over-appreciate our spouses. We can all use more appreciation. For many of us, our time at work mentally, physically, and emotionally depletes us and cause us to feel poorly about ourselves. What a blessing it is to have a home that functions as a sanctuary filled with appreciation.

A Healthy Relationship

As we conclude this section on generosity, let's look at what Scripture has to say about generosity:

"Remember this: The person who sows sparingly will also reap sparingly, and the person who sows generously will also reap generously. 7 Each person should do as he has decided in his heart—not reluctantly or out of necessity, for God loves a cheerful giver" (2 Corinthians 9:6).

"Give, and you will receive. Your gift will return to you in full—pressed down, shaken together to make room for more, running over, and poured into your lap. The amount you give will determine the amount you get back" (Luke 6:38).

"The generous will prosper; those who refresh others will themselves be refreshed" (Prov. 11:25).

ROMANCE

Here's a quick question: Who reads the most romance novels? Need a hint? Really?

Answer: Women.

If this comes as a surprise to any of our male readers, we need to talk. The fact that women purchase millions of romance novels every year is just one indication of a very significant fact—romance is important to women.

Why did we stop doing what caused us to fall in love in the first place?

For many of us, romance was a special part of our dating and courtship. Flowers, endless personal conversations, and quiet walks were strokes on the canvases of our new relationships. Somehow, though, time and the busyness of life—work, children, and responsibilities—have caused what was sweet and intimate to fall by the wayside. Why did we stop doing what caused us to fall in love in the first place? Life sometimes gets in the way of romance, but we can't and shouldn't let it go. No matter how long we've been married, it should remain a vital part of our relationship.

Romance doesn't have to involve jetting off to Tuscany for the weekend or rescuing our mates from the jaws of a mutant alligator (I think I just got an idea for a romance novel). It can be simple, yet still be thoughtful.

Here are a few thoughts to keep the romance alive in our marriages:

Romance begins with words and starts outside the bedroom, not in it.

Contrary to what many think, romance begins with words and starts outside the bedroom, not in it. This is especially true for women.

Husbands, then, should be intentional about talking to our wives in the morning or at lunch before we come rolling in for the evening. We can also be intentional about planning a date, whether it's dinner and a movie or a surprise weekend out of town. When we thoughtfully plan, it tells our wives they are important enough to warrant thinking ahead about our time together.

This is quite a contrast to the way we often approach romance:

I feel that my wife is bugging me to take here somewhere. I begrudgingly get into the car, turn to her, and say, "All right, where do you want to go?"

She responds in frustration, "I don't care, just anywhere."

My defense is, "but I asked her where she wanted to go!"

Yes, I did. However, how much more thoughtful would it have been if I'd approached her early in the day with the proposition, "Hey, Honey, how about just you and me head out for a bite after work? I'd really like to be alone with you."

What lady wouldn't respond to that invitation with an excited *yes?*

If I wanted to take it to the next level, I could plan where to go before I picked her up. Even make reservations if needed. Having a plan and investing time and thought communicates to our wives that they are valuable, important, and worth thinking and planning

60

for our time together.

When we demonstrate thoughtfulness in this way, our wives begin to think about us and how much they want to be with us. It sets the tone for our time together before it even begins.

Romance doesn't have to be fancy or expensive. Light a few candles and cook together or order in a nice meal. Put on some music. Spend a few meaningful moments over a glass of your favorite beverage while looking into each other's eyes. Freshen up your bedtime wardrobe with a trip to your favorite lingerie shop. Take a scented bath; there are some great smelling products for both men and women. Put on cologne or perfume. The simplest things can often bring the greatest rewards.

Sometimes romance is as simple as asking your spouse what means the most to them. As Dr. Gary Chapman explains in his bestselling book *The Five Love Languages*, there are five ways in which we receive love from someone: through words of affirmation, quality time, acts of service, gift giving, and physical touch.[3] Reading resources like this book communicates you are intentional about your marriage. I highly recommend the book in order to discover how to speak your spouse's love language.

When we intentionally focus on our spouses, we let them know that nothing and no one else matters but them. Now that's romance.

INTIMACY

Quick … what's the first word that comes to your mind when you think of intimacy?

If it's *sex*, you're probably a man.

If it's *closeness* or *emotional connection*, you're probably a woman.

These different responses spotlight the disconnect between the sexes over the matter of intimacy. As we examine the full scope of intimacy, we might be surprised to see that it's really fairly simple. God designed intimacy to contain three parts: body, soul & spirit.

A Healthy Relationship

_____

Sometimes romance is as simple as asking your spouse what means the most to them.

_____

Intimacy on a soul level also includes how we think about ourselves, each other, and our relationship.

We begin with the soul because intimacy begins in the mind. The word *soul* comes from the Latin and Greek word *psyche,* the place from which we get the word *psychology.* The soul is the seat of belief—our mind and thoughts. It is also the place for feelings, desires, affections, and emotional intimacy.

Because not everyone is comfortable sharing feelings and emotions, this part of intimacy can be challenging. True emotional intimacy, however, requires that we share our deepest thoughts, feelings and desires. Healthy relationships are always characterized by a willingness to trust each other.

Sharing deeply is typically easier for females than males, but a determined husband can overcome his tendency to be emotionally reserved. Connecting emotionally is especially important for women. This is why the ever-popular romance novel is always packed with emotional events such as conflict, victory, or rescue.

Keep in mind that our relationships don't have to be fraught with drama in order for us to be emotionally attached. Connecting as soul mates means being able to share our feelings honestly, authentically, and without inhibition.

We must be intentional to connect through words and emotions.

Intimacy on a soul level also includes how we think about ourselves, each other, and our relationship. Our thoughts and beliefs are powerful directors in how we live. How we think about ourselves can either give us confidence or cause us to operate from a position of low self-esteem. Low self-esteem can greatly challenge a relationship.

I (Dennis) frequently work with people who have struggled with low self-esteem for years. Their stories consistently demonstrate that how a person views himself often becomes a self-fulfilling prophecy, thus perpetuating his perception that he is a failure. For those who regularly feel this way, talking with a professional counselor can be very helpful. He or she can help a person see him/herself the way God sees him/her, which is anything but negative.

How we see each other is equally important. If we see our spouses as controlling, manipulative or demeaning, we won't feel safe enough be intimate at any level. If we think of our spouses as loving, caring, and supportive, we'll be more willing to be open and honest.

How we think about our relationships is also vital. If we think of our marriages as traps, dead ends, or a hard work, we'll not be as willing to invest the time and effort it needs to make it better. If we think of our relationships as gifts, blessings, and wonderful, this will greatly influence our emotional connections.

Intimacy for woman begins in the soul realm—with words, thoughts, ideas, dreams, and desires. To bond intimately with our wives, we must exchange this type of communication with them. This can be especially challenging for men, because male intimacy begins with visual stimulation, which leads to thoughts, which eventually leads to action.

So in order to fan the flames of intimacy within our marriages, we must be intentional to connect through words and emotions in an environment of honesty and authenticity. Intimacy begins in the soul.

THE BODY—SEXUAL INTIMACY

Sex is what usually comes to mind when we think of intimacy, but let's be clear—sex is not intimacy. We can have intimacy without sex, and we can have sex without intimacy. When we have intimacy and sex, now this is awesome.

We noted that soul intimacy begins in the brain. The same is true for physical intimacy. It begins with how we think about ourselves, our mates, and our relationship.

Because God wired men to be visually stimulated, sex for them begins with a vision. That vision generates thought, which leads to a physical reaction, which then leads to action.

For women, sex is the result of an emotional connection. As we said earlier, words, moods, and thoughts all play into the intimate

63

experience. The sexual act for her is a culmination of all these things. This why it's been said in many different ways that men are microwaves and women are slow cookers.

A man can be putting out fires all day at work, have to change a flat tire on the way home, drop his favorite coffee mug walking into the house, but still be ready for sex when he walks through the door.

For a woman, everything she experiences through the day contributes to her mood. She may have had a run in with her boss, spilled something on her clothes, worried about a stray dog on the side of the road, and fretted about a bill prior seeing her husband. Before she can even think about the physical act of intimacy, she must have time, attention, and understanding to process everything that has happened during her day.

Physical intimacy is also about being comfortable with both our bodies and our mate's bodies. It's about feeling secure enough share with them what we desire and what pleases us.

It's important to note that it is not okay to demand of our mates what they may find uncomfortable, painful, or embarrassing. I (Dennis) have encountered many men who will use I Corinthians 7:3-5 as a way to demand this of their wives:

"The husband should fulfill his wife's sexual needs, and the wife should fulfill her husband's needs. The wife gives authority over her body to her husband, and the husband gives authority over his body to his wife. Do not deprive each other of sexual relations, unless you both agree to refrain from sexual intimacy for a limited time so you can give yourselves more completely to prayer. Afterward, you should come together again so that Satan won't be able to tempt you because of your lack of self-control." (NLT)

We should never use sex as a weapon, withhold it as punishment, or demand it by the law of Scripture. In all things, God calls us to operate in love and respect toward each other. Remember—we are not our own (I Cor. 6:19). We first belong to God, and then to each other.

As husband and wife, we have a tremendous opportunity to join together not only as soul mates and intimate lovers, but also as spiritual partners in the Kingdom. Matthew 19:5 tells us that a man and his wife are *"united into one."*

A Healthy Relationship

What does this spiritual intimacy look like, and why is it important?

The first connection in spiritual intimacy is our personal relationship with God. It's this communion with the intimate God that restores our souls, heals to our hearts, and fills us with love only the Father can give. This vibrant intimacy prepares us to love each other as God designed.

Spiritual intimacy within a marriage involves a union of belief.

Spiritual intimacy within a marriage involves a union of belief.

This union of belief translates, according to Deuteronomy 32:30, as the difference between one person's ability to chase 1,000 enemies to a unified couple's ability to chase 10,000.

Obviously the effectiveness of two people walking in unity of belief is huge. For a married couple, this type of unity means being open to becoming everything God desires them to be.

If one spouse is an unbeliever, this presents a challenge. It's encouraging to note, however, that according to I Peter 3:1-2 an unbelieving husband can be won by observing the Godly lifestyle of his wife. This text specifically mentions the instruction to win him over "without words," so no sermons.

It's important for both spouses to agree on where you will worship and serve. "Can two people walk together without agreeing on the direction?" (Amos 3:3 NLT). A divided house can be challenging in any area, and this can include attending different churches. Keep in mind that agreeing doesn't mean one spouse gets to decide. Instead, it means we arrive at a decision based on mutual agreement (more about this in the next chapter).

Spending time praying for each other and with each other is also vital in developing spiritual unity. If there are areas where a couple is struggling to agree, praying for and with each other can help. Never underestimate the power of praying together.

I (Dennis) remember feeling intimidated when my girlfriend (now my wife) would pray before and after dates. She seemed to have a relationship with God I didn't have. I determined I would press through any fear of embarrassment, and, with time, I became very confident in praying with her.

It's a wonderful feeling to be able to discuss the Word of God with your spouse, pray with each other, and enjoy the presence of the Lord together. Experiencing the presence of God with each other is a beautiful expression of spiritual intimacy. It also brings a sense of security and protection to our marriages.

Spending time praying for each other and with each other is also vital in developing spiritual unity.

CHAPTER 8

BE INTENTIONAL ABOUT . . .

RELATIONAL SUCCESS

---

4 RULES FOR RELATIONSHIPS

Rules aren't always negative. Many times they function as guardrails to keep us on the road and enjoying life. In the marriage context, rules can mean standards by which we conduct our relationships.

Dr. Willard F. Harley, Jr., in his book *Surviving An Affair*, lists four rules for marital recovery. I believe these same rules are excellent for preventing an affair from ever developing. Harley's four rules are:

> *The Rule of Honesty*
> *The Rule of Protection*
> *The Rule of Care*
> *The Rule of Time*[1]

THE RULE OF HONESTY

"Be totally open and honest with your spouse." [2]

One of the most common conversations I have with couples is when one or both spouses say they're afraid to be honest. Their comments sound like this:

"I'm afraid she'll be mad."

"I don't want to hurt his feelings."

Honesty is crucial if the relationship is to be authentic.

67

"I just end up not saying anything in order to keep the peace."

I often hear comments like these from those who don't like confrontation. They think honesty isn't an option if they want to keep the peace. Honesty, however, is crucial if the relationship is to be authentic.

Harley writes that there are five parts to cultivating honesty with our spouses: emotional honesty, historical honesty, current honesty, future honesty, and complete honesty.[3] Let's look at each one.

Emotional honesty

"Reveal your emotional reactions- both positive and negative- to the events of your life, particularly to your spouse's behavior." [4]

I've heard many couples say they're afraid of hurting the other's feelings, so rather than cause harm, they shut down or are not honest with their feelings. Harley points out that negative reactions are important because they are a signal that something is wrong.

"Honesty enables couples to make appropriate adjustments to each other, and adjustment is what a good marriage is all about,"[5] Harley says. Rather than ignore the negative feelings, this is an opportunity to examine what's wrong.

Historical honesty

"Reveal information about your personal history, particularly events that demonstrate personal weakness or failure." [6]

If we enter a relationship pretending, it will be an exhausting way to live.

By being honest, we can experience one of life's greatest joys--to be loved and accepted despite known weaknesses or past mistakes. We should never pretend to be someone we're not. If we enter a relationship pretending, it will be an exhausting way to live. At some point, we'll grow tired of pretending, and we certainly don't want our spouses to find out about our past from someone else. Today is the day to begin to be honest about past victories and failures.

Current honesty

"Reveal information about the events of your day. Provide your spouse with a calendar of your activities, with special emphasis on those that may affect your spouse." [7]

In my marriage, Susan and I talk about the events of our day. It's important to include our spouses in the day-to-day activities of our lives for several reasons.

Providing our spouses with an idea of our activities for the day or week gives them security and comfort. We keep separate calendars, but usually talk about our schedules on a daily basis. We may discuss what's on the schedule for that day as well as what's coming up in the future. Most days, we just ask each other about what's on the calendar. It helps to know where our spouses intend to be during the day in case of emergency. Finally, knowing each other's schedules helps promote accountability.

If we withhold information from our spouses, they begin to experience doubt and suspicion. Seeking to be above board in our daily routines can prevent this possible anxiety.

Future honesty

"Reveal your thoughts and plans regarding future activities and objectives." [8]

When we fail to tell our spouses about our plans, we're not being honest. Most people don't like surprises, except at Christmas and birthdays. Keeping plans to ourselves doesn't build trust. Talking about what we're thinking, planning, or expecting does. If we're planning to go on a golf trip, we should check it out with our spouse before she notices that our clubs are gone and so are we. Guys, if we're planning to go on a golf trip, we should check it out with our spouse before she notices that our clubs are gone and so are we. Ladies, when your friends call for a "Girl's Night Out", it's courteous to share your plans with your husband before committing.

Some of us try to use the mantra, *It's better to ask for forgiveness than permission.* What I've described isn't about asking for permission or forgiveness; it's about being thoughtful and courteous.

Complete Honesty

"Do not leave your spouse with a false impression about your thoughts, feelings, habits, likes, dislikes, personal history, daily activities, or plans for the future. Do not deliberately keep personal information from your spouse." [9]

The best approach is to create an environment that encourages transparency.

If we are to feel comfortable sharing our thoughts and feelings honestly, it helps to have a safety agreement in place. Couples should commit to avoid angry outbursts, disrespect, and demands when sharing with each other. If we exhibit angry outbursts every time our spouses share honestly, then they will be less likely to speak honestly with us in the future.

The best approach is to create an environment that encourages transparency. We do this by being open to honest communication without threat or anger. If you ever feel in danger of abuse, separate from your spouse until you're confident of being able to safely and honestly share your thoughts with them.

Keep in mind that if we haven't operated in complete honesty up to this point in our relationships, it's going to take a lot of courage to change this. Prepare for some challenging conversations, but take heart. It's still the healthy thing to do.

The Importance of Authenticity

I'm just keeping it real. There's a lot of truth to this statement. Posers have no place in healthy relationships. Authenticity, however, is much more than just being real. It's being honest with ourselves first. Unless we're honest with ourselves, it's difficult to be honest with others. It's also hard for others to respect us unless we're being authentic. The longer we're married, the more we come to know

70

each other. Because of this, our spouses are usually the first to know if we're not being authentic.

I (Dennis) remember preaching a great sermon years ago. Afterward, my wife confronted me by saying, "You were telling people to do something you're not doing." After I moved past feeling angry at her comment, the Lord convicted me of not being authentic. Today, one of my main goals in life is to walk the talk.

Relational Success

Just like it takes a lot of courage to be honest, it also takes a lot of courage to be authentic. But unless we want a relationship built on a lie, we must strive to be real.

THE RULE OF PROTECTION

If someone was trying to break into our house, we'd defend our family at any cost, yet when it comes to protecting each other as husband and wife, we often feel the freedom to say or do just about anything without even considering the damage it causes.

Protect your spouse from anything we might do to cause them harm.

Protecting each other from outside sources seems like a no brainer. Protecting each other *from* each other may not seem as necessary, but just like it's important to protect our families from intruders, it's also important to protect your spouses from anything we might do to cause them harm.

Here's a very important way to protect our spouses—avoid being the cause of their pain. This means anything we do or say that hurts them. Does this mean we never share the truth? Of course not. There's a difference in speaking the truth in love (see Chapter 3) and shouting the truth in anger. One way brings clarity and understanding; the other can cause much damage.

Harley lists the three most common ways we cause our spouses pain: angry outbursts, disrespectful judgments, and selfish demands.[10]

If we follow our instincts, we'll hurt each other every time.

"When anger wins, love loses."[11] Have you ever heard the saying, *You may have won the battle but you've lost the war?* We may win the argument, but at what cost to our relationship? On the flipside, are you willing to lose an argument in favor of finding a solution to the issue? Anger is a horrible way to communicate anything. Anger relies on intimidation to make a point. In most cases, anger causes a reaction rather than a response. Anger, which is an emotion, breeds emotion. If we follow our instincts, we'll hurt each other every time.

Disrespectful judgments

We can also cause our spouses pain by trying to impose a system of values and beliefs upon them. We might use statements like: *That's just the way it is,* or *It's my way or the highway,* or *This is how things are going to be around here.*

When we use words like these, what we're trying to do is straighten them out. Whether we actually say it or not, we're probably thinking that our spouses don't know what they're talking about, and it's our responsibility to point this out.

While it's okay to disagree, it's not okay to completely disregard our spouse's opinions and berate them as if they were stupid. When we disagree, we must do so respectfully.

Typically our conversation goes south when we feel threatened by our spouse's opinion. When this occurs, we attempt to ram our point down the other's throat. Sometimes we attempt to further demean them by calling names.

We can avoid a disrespectful judgment by being willing to discuss an issue without being judgmental and disrespectful.

Selfish demands

Demands carry a threat of punishment. *If you refuse me, you'll regret it.*

This sets an unhealthy pattern for a relationship. Fear never breeds anything good in a relationship. If we have to make demands of our spouses, we're probably feeling very insecure and threatened.

When one spouse wins and the other loses, our marriage always loses. When we demand instead of ask, we set the stage for a win or lose situation. This breeds an unhealthy marriage and perpetuates a dysfunctional relationship.

Demands do not encourage people to cooperate; they drain deposits from our love accounts. If we picture each spouse as having a love bank that can be added to or withdrawn from, we see that demands deplete any positive investments we've made in our relationship. If the pattern continues, our marriages begin to suffer under the deficit, much like an overdrawn bank account. And we all know that when our bank account is overdrawn, we are in serious trouble.

So how do we successfully navigate marital negotiations? By being thoughtful.

It's difficult to be thoughtful when it means we may not get what we want. Being thoughtful means being considerate of the other person, which can be a scary proposition for someone who is used to being the center of attention. Remember that in a relationship, there are two people involved. Each person is equally valuable, and their desires, needs, and wants are equally valuable.

A great way to approach a discussion in which we want to consider our spouses and their desires is to ask the question, *How would you feel* _____?

Here's how this works: Suppose we've been offered a promotion. The promotion, however, involves moving to another state. Before we give our boss an answer, we request time to talk it over with our spouse. Believe it or not, there are some who would immediately take an offer like this without ever consulting their spouses. We call them divorced people.

So we head home excited about the opportunity and tell our spouse that we have some great news. As we sit down at the kitchen table, we begin by saying, "How would you feel about moving to Florida? I've just been offered a promotion."

This approach doesn't guarantee our spouse will agree or be excited about the opportunity, but it does demonstrate that we're not attempting to be selfish or demanding. Instead, we're making every attempt to thoughtfully consider our spouse's feelings.

THE RULE OF CARE

"Meet your spouse's most important emotional needs." [12]

Sometimes it's easier to mow the grass, wash dishes, or go to work than to think about meeting our spouse's emotional needs. These other activities don't require intimacy, and intimacy scares some of us. In any healthy relationship, intimacy is much more than just the physical sexual act—it's tapping into our emotions.

Becoming an expert on each other is an intentional investment we make in our relationships.

In my experience, when a woman has an affair, it begins with an emotional connection. This emotional affair meets an internal need she has that surpasses anything external. When a man has an affair, it's not as likely to be based on an emotional need, but a desire to be respected. Focusing on each other's top five emotional needs can help us have awesome marriages.

So how do we protect our relationship and meet each other's most important emotional needs?

Identify the most important emotional needs.

How do we do this? We ask. Only our spouse can tell us where to put our greatest relational efforts. We start by asking our spouses to list their top five emotional needs. As they do, we must promise not to defend or argue with any of the needs they list.

Here's an example. Suppose my wife lists a need for affection as one of her top five. When I read this, I could immediately begin justifying and defending myself. "What do you mean; I'm not affectionate with you? I'm always hugging and touching you. Don't you remember last night when ..."

74

If I look at it from her perspective, I realize she's not saying I'm not affectionate; she's just saying affection is a priority to her. It might also be helpful to ask, "What does affection look like to you?" While my idea of affection might be squeezing the life out of her as soon as I get home, she might instead prefer a gentle caress.

Once each of us lists our top five emotional needs, it's time to go through the list with each other and ask the next question, which can be a little scary, "Are you satisfied with the way I'm meeting this need?"

If the answer *is no*, then ask, "How would you like for me to meet this need?" Phrasing it in a positive light invites a positive suggestion, which is much more encouraging than criticism. Criticism sounds like this: "I don't like it when you ..." A positive suggestion says, "I would love it if you would ..."

Becoming an expert on each other is an intentional investment we make in our relationships. As we become experts in meeting each other's needs, our efforts will begin paying big dividends. Harley agrees. "Learning to meet each other's emotional needs in marriage is far less complicated than going through the agonizing ritual of affairs and divorce." [13]

THE RULE OF TIME

There is no substitute for time. Matthew 6:21 reminds us, "Wherever your treasure is, there the desires of your heart will also be." Wherever we invest as a couple is where we'll reap the rewards. Couples frequently sit in my office shaking their heads, wondering how they grew apart. When I probe a little deeper, I usually find they simply haven't made together time a priority.

Spending time in the same house is not the same as spending time together.

Spending time in the same house is not the same as spending time together. Oh, they may spend many hours in the same place, but instead of intentionally interacting with each other, they work, watch movies, check social networking sites, or wrestle to get the kids bathed and in bed. Make no mistake, family time is important.

So is time with friends, but time alone, just the two of you, is vital and rewarding.

Taking time with our spouses means intentionally scheduling time together. Planning time together may not sound romantic, but the thoughtfulness of planning combined with the anticipation of being together will set the stage for a very satisfying experience.

Let's think back to the beginning of our relationships, when we had to schedule a day and time to see each other. It was called a date, and dates should still have a place on our calendars. It's also important, when we're together, to be sure we're not multi-tasking. We should give our spouses our undivided attention. This means looking each other in the eyes. A friend shared that his dad taught him to hold hands with his sweetheart and look deeply into her eyes. This was a way to ensure that he focused totally on her.

Today's world likes to tell us that multi-tasking is an efficient way to do business. Studies now show the opposite—multi-tasking actually reduces our effectiveness. [14] And even if it didn't, we're not talking about business. We're talking about our most important human relationships, not a results-driven corporation.

We each have emotional needs that require our spouse's un-divided attention. This is why it's important to schedule time to be together without children, relatives, or friends. Some couples hesitate to leave their children with a relative or sitter. They feel guilty about not including them in every outing they plan.

Children derive their greatest sense of security from the stable, strong relationship between their parents.

What these couples fail to understand is that children derive their greatest sense of security from the stable, strong relationship between their parents. When we spend time together, away from our children, we help build this relationship.

Consider it an investment in the health of our families every time you get away for a regular date night or weekend. If you feel you need permission for the two of you to go on a date or week-end together, then consider this your permission! Your children will survive, and you'll be a much better couple because of it. A couple that invests time in each other is much happier, which, in

76

turn, creates a healthier climate for their children and their family.

As we plan our dates, we should intentionally seek activities that will help us meet the emotional needs of our spouses. If my wife expresses a desire for uninterrupted talk time, we might go to a coffee shop and sip lattes. If I feel like I need more affection, we might put the kids to bed early or ask grandparents or trusted friends to keep the kids for a night. Sometimes a simple walk in the park can make a huge deposit in our relationship. As I've mentioned before, Susan and I frequently take a walk either in the morning or evening. It gives us a chance to exercise, check in with other, and pray together.

To have a healthy marriage, we must be intentional about spending time together.

THE POLICY OF JOINT AGREEMENT

The final standard Harley has produced to help couples manage their relationship in a healthy manner is the Policy of Joint Agreement. He describes it this way:

"If something you want to do is not agreeable to your spouse, the Policy of Joint Agreement offers your spouse protection. Following the Policy means that if something you want to do very much would hurt your spouse, you won't do it." [15]

This is crucial when we discuss future plans. In our own marriage, we have agreed to use this policy for most major decisions. By following this policy, both spouses agree that major decisions (changing jobs, moving, major purchases, etc.) will be made only after both parties have talked, prayed, and come to an agreement.

What if we can't agree? Under the rules of the Policy of Agreement, if we can't come to an agreement, we don't act until we do.

Suppose one of us gets an offer for a promotion, but it requires moving 100 miles away. If my wife and I can't agree after talking, praying, and seeking counsel, then we choose not to act.

Many times in our 30+ years of marriage, we've had to make a major decision. Unfortunately, we haven't always employed the Policy of Mutual Agreement. Without mutual agreement, we overlooked a possible accountability and safety net that could have protected us from disastrous results.

Employing the Policy of Joint Agreement also gives us both time to pray, discuss, and consider the effects or consequences of our decisions. This creates an atmosphere of respect for each other and establishes accountability for the family.

CHAPTER 9

BE INTENTIONAL ABOUT...

ENJOYMENT

A word I commonly use with couples I counsel is *work*. Relationships and marriages require work. Our health requires work. Communication requires work. It's important to remember, however, that life doesn't have to be all work.

Marriage and relationships can and should be a lot of fun. After all, we're spending our lives with the people we love most in the world. Yet even fun requires being intentional. For marriages that have lost the fun and feel more like an obligation, this chapter is full of practical insight on how to bring the enjoyment back into your marriages.

DATES

Let's define *dates*. Dates are just what the word implies—an intentional time set aside to focus attention on each other. Some of Susan and my favorite dates include: watching a movie, eating at our favorite restaurant (or a new one if we're feeling adventurous), or going out of town for a long weekend.

We've often found that unless we intentionally put a day and time on the calendar, our lives fill up, almost by default, with other commitments and other people.

Couples frequently tell me (Dennis) that they can't afford a date, don't have time, can't find a babysitter, etc. These are the same reasons why we don't exercise, save money, etc. While on the

Our dates aren't about spending money or impressing anybody; they're about spending time together.

surface these reasons may hold some truth, we all know that the old adage, *We find a way to do what we really want to do*, applies here.

So, just for fun, let's take a moment to address some of the excuses we use for not going on dates with our spouses:

NO MONEY

Dates don't have to cost a lot of money. If we're creative, they may not cost anything. Here are some fun, inexpensive ways to spend time together: How about making sandwiches and heading to the park for a picnic? Depending on where you live, you may even be able to walk there (two for one: exercise and time together). You could ride bikes or walk (win-win—exercise and time together). What about sitting in the backyard with a cup of coffee around the fire pit? Here's another: Susan and I have had some good laughs riding in my old truck to the farmer's market or to the home improvement store for mulch. Remember, our dates aren't about spending money or impressing anybody; they're about spending time together.

NO BABYSITTER

This can be a real challenge, especially if we have more than one child or don't live near relatives. We've been in this situation. We lived a thousand miles away from family when our children were young. It's from experience, then, that I say it's not impossible to spend a night or a weekend away.

Ask a trusted friend at church or at work for a favor. Talk with other parents and offer to take turns watching each other's children. As you get to know people, you may find other parents in the same situation as you are who would welcome the opportunity to exchange childcare.

If the truth be told, this is generally not a problem of time, but of priority. We're all busy with work, school activities, and church commitments. We all have the same amount of time. Moses, Jesus, George Washington, and Albert Einstein all shared the limits of a 24-hour day.

Every day we make time to eat, dress, play, and work. We give attention to the activities and relationships that are most important to us. The further down our list of priorities an activity or relationship is, the more likely we will neglect or overlook it.

Prioritizing time together says to the world that our marriages add to the quality of our lives. The intentional investment of time is a proactive way to prevent future marriage disasters.

While spontaneity and creativity come naturally to some, others have to learn them. Sometimes a fun date can be as simple as building a fire in the fire pit on a chilly evening after you've put the kids to bed. Even something as mundane as a trip to the store for supplies can become a great time for laughter and togetherness.

Remember, dates are simply intentional times spent together. What we do when we're together is far less important than simply being together. So let's be intentional about it.

GOOD HUMOR

Humor is important in any relationship. Many women, when asked what qualities they value most in a man, list *makes me laugh* as one of the most desirable. Thankfully, we don't have to be a comedian to be good humored. And while some people express humor more naturally than others, we can all be lighthearted enough to enjoy a good laugh.

Keep in mind that everything doesn't have to be a joke. In fact, some people take humor to an extreme, which causes a different problem. (Imagine what it would be like to live with Robin

81

Williams.) We can, however, be intentionally cheerful in our interactions with each other.

Keep in mind that it's never OK to get a laugh at our spouse's expense. This type of humor often stems from a desire to feel accepted by those around us. And while it's okay to make fun of ourselves, throwing each other under the bus in public to get a laugh can seriously damage our relationship. While our spouses may initially laugh along, they'll hurt on the inside and struggle to feel safe around us.

I'm not talking about being a prude and never seeing the humor in life. As a couple, Susan and I have a great time joking and enjoying the antics of our family. Because we've invested in each other in positive ways, we know that kidding is not meant to be hurtful. We are, however, mindful to protect each other's feelings and will often ask if anything we said or did felt hurtful.

It's always wise to guard our spouse's feelings and stay away from anything that might be disrespectful. A laugh at our spouse's expense is a high cost to pay for a moment's pleasure.

Just as everything doesn't have to be a joke, so everything doesn't have to be serious. Look for ways to release laughter. Laughter releases endorphins that can actually bring healing.

Some of us are not naturally able to see the humor in everyday life. If this is the case, deliberately watch a funny movie or TV show together. Pull out the old family videos (or DVDs if you recorded in this century) and laugh!

Proverbs 17:22 reminds us, "A cheerful heart is good medicine."

GRATEFULNESS

Gratitude costs us nothing, but lends great value to our marriages and relationships.

One of the greatest mistakes we make in relationships is to become so accustomed to each other that we take each other for granted. In the midst of our busy and complicated lives, we get into the mode of "plowing with our heads down" just to make it through another day. In contrast, to be grateful is to daily and intentionally appreciate each other.

82

Being grateful involves taking a look at our lives, and in this case our marriages, through the lens of thankfulness. Is our marriage everything we want? Probably not. Is it everything we need? Maybe not, but we can begin by giving thanks for what it is.

This may mean speaking appreciation to each other in simple ways like:

I sure appreciate how hard you work every day.

I'm so thankful to have you in my life.

You are a wonderful mom to our children.

Thank you for keeping the grass cut.

Being grateful is giving thanks for the blessings we already have. This intentional action of gratitude costs us nothing, but lends great value to our marriages and relationships.

CHAPTER 10

BE INTENTIONAL ABOUT...

SPIRITUAL LIFE

A powerful effect of drawing closer to God is that we'll also draw closer to each other.

We examined some aspects of sharing spiritual life together in Chapter 5 as we examined spiritual intimacy in the context of a healthy relationship. In this chapter, we'll look at how being on the same page spiritually can add depth and dimension to our marriages. A powerful effect of drawing closer to God is that we'll also draw closer to each other. Sharing spiritual life with our spouses includes praying, worshipping, and serving together.

PRAY TOGETHER

"One puts a thousand to flight ... two, put ten thousand to flight ... " (*Deut. 32:30*).

It still amazes me (Dennis) when couples share that they rarely pray together. It especially boggles my mind when a minister and his spouse say they don't usually pray together. When I ask why, I get a variety of reasons:

Praying with each other brings togetherness, security, and power to our relationship.

One will point to the other and say, "He/she doesn't want to."

Or, "I never really thought about it."

Or perhaps, "By the time we're finished eating, get the kids bathed, and get ourselves into bed, there's no time."

One man shared that he felt his wife was critical of him when he prayed. I gently reminded him that he was talking to God, not his wife, and God would listen and not criticize.

Susan and I frequently pray together, either in the morning or

84

the evening, as we walk in the neighborhood. Sometimes one of us will call the other during the day to request prayer for a situation at work. Our children know if they share any concerns with us, we'll pray with them on the spot. At night, before we nod off to sleep, we'll again pray together briefly. While praying together seemed awkward at first, the more we did it, the more natural it became.

Praying with each other brings togetherness, security, and power to our relationship. It strengthens the bond between us and makes it more difficult for the enemy to invade.

WORSHIP TOGETHER

We all should have a personal relationship with God that includes our own worship/quiet time with Him. This brings strength and substance to both our personal lives and our marriage. It's also important, however, that we worship together. I'm often surprised at the couples who don't attend the same church. Oftentimes, this means they hold different core beliefs.

Choosing to worship together builds oneness, strengthens unity, and helps us be like-minded in other areas of our lives.

If you and your spouse are struggling with which church to attend, pray together for God's direction and confirmation. Keep in mind that there is no perfect church, so expecting to find everything you're looking for in a church body is unrealistic. As you visit churches, take time to pray and ask God to help you agree on what the essentials are. Ask yourself, *what are the most important core beliefs for me and my family?*

While attending church together is important, keep in mind that worship can take other forms as well. We can share a concert, a message on TV, or even a good book. Sharing the Word with each other as God speaks to us in our quiet times can also be a great way to encourage each other and build spiritual unity. These various forms of worship allow us to come together and experience the presence of God as a couple.

Working together for the kingdom of God is an important component of spiritual bonding. The time we spend accomplishing a task or fulfilling a mission is invaluable in creating unity, both with our spouses and with other believers. As we find a group of people to do life with (friendships) and a spiritual body to connect with (our church), it's also crucial that we find our place of service.

As we serve together as a couple, we create stronger bonds and experience a greater sense of purpose.

Many churches and ministries offer spiritual gift assessments to help members discover how God has created and gifted them to serve. Since God gives us these gifts, it is our privilege and responsibility to share them with others. Be mindful of the fact that God may have given each of you different spiritual gifts. Ask Him where and when to use these gifts to serve, both individually and together.

As we serve together as a couple, we create stronger bonds and experience a greater sense of purpose. This sense of mission is important as we develop unity and find our place in the world.

CHAPTER 11

BE INTENTIONAL ABOUT...

THE MARRIAGE COVENANT

CONTRACT VS. COVENANT

One of the most unfortunate consequences of an increasingly litigious society has been the evolution of marriage from what God intended it to be—a covenant—into a very cold, business-oriented contract. One of the misconceptions I (Dennis) hear frequently is that "marriage is an agreement." While the state does require a legal document to officially recognize a union for benefits, etc., there are many couples who have conducted their relationships primarily as a legal agreement. Since, by definition, a contract is a legal agreement, this has led many marriages to function under a contract mentality.

Let's look first at what this legal agreement we call marriage contains and how it operates.

CONTRACT

In its truest form, a contract is an "agreement with specific terms between two or more persons or entities in which there is a promise to do something in return for a valuable benefit known as consideration."

Based on the contract design for marriage then, a marriage is an agreement between two consenting parties.

If and when this agreement is broken, these are the provisions of the termination:

A contract contains provision for *breach of contract*. A breach of contract is a violation by either party to perform contractual obligations or the interference of the other party's performance. When this takes place, the offended party has the right to sue for damages. So if you or your spouse don't perform your contractual obligations, then you can be sued (or in this case, divorced).

A contract may also contain a provision for *breach of trust*. The breach of trust is defined as any act or omission on the part of the trustee which is inconsistent with the terms of the trust agreement or the law of trusts. This typically involves the misuse in some way of money or property. So under this provision, if you or your spouse don't handle your assets to the satisfaction of the other, you could be held liable. Again, if this contract is broken in some way, compensation is due.

A contractual view of marriage is the reason for prenuptial agreements. A prenuptial agreement (prenup) is typically put in place before a marriage when the parties involved are concerned about their rights to property and finances in the event of a divorce. *In other words, this is preplanning for a divorce.* In some people's opinion, this makes for good financial/practical sense. *If this marriage doesn't work out,* they think, *we have an exit plan in place.* It also makes it easier to leave the relationship, instead of work through the issues. Although it may make practical and financial sense, a prenuptial agreement undermines the relationship.

None of this sounds very romantic, does it? In simple terms, a contract marriage says, *I will keep my promise to you as long as you keep your promise to me.*

A contract marriage says, "I will keep my promise to you as long as you keep your promise to me."

This mentality leads a couple to keep a mental score sheet or, as the old saying goes, *tit for tat*. It's all about keeping score. If the wife went and bought a new dress this week, then her husband decides it's okay to get a new golf club. Never mind that they may not be able to afford either, it's all about what's fair.

When couples keep score, their relationships are characterized by a strong sense of entitlement. There is a constant struggle to maintain *what's mine* and *what's fair*. Never mind what's right. What's more important, at this point, is not losing.

A contract is about rules and regulations. I've counseled couples who have actually written out rules for their relationship:

We will have sex three times a week.

We will visit your mom once a month.

You may go on one golfing trip per year with the guys.

In a contract type of marriage, both parties are bound by the law in how they conduct the relationship, there are penalties for breaking the agreement, and there are rules to follow in order for it to be fair.

A COVENANT

A covenant is different.

A covenant is God's design for marriage. In a covenant marriage, the relationship is based on a vow. A vow is stronger than a contract. During the marriage ceremony, the couple makes a vow before God and man. Vows are the declaration of one party to the other.

A covenant is not about rules and regulations, it's about rela-

When couples keep score, their relationships are characterized by a strong sense of entitlement.

A covenant is not about rules and regulations, it's about relationship.

89

tionship. We don't love our spouses because a contract dictates we must; we love your spouses because we've declared and vowed to nurture our relationship.

A covenant is about hope.

"I will keep my promise even if you don't, because I've made a vow to God, not just to you."

Without a covenant relationship with Christ, Paul says "You lived in this world without God and without hope" (Eph. 2:12). "Without a covenant relationship with your spouse, your marriage is without hope," writes Dr. Fred Lowery, author of the book *Covenant Marriage — Staying Together for Life*. A covenant-less marriage is a marriage without God. If our marriages are Godless, then all hope could be lost. If all hope is lost, then divorce is inevitable, because something is bound to happen one day that will threaten our relationship.

A marriage without a covenant is a duet, but God designed marriage to be a trio. Ecclesiastes 4:12 tells us, "... a threefold cord is not easily broken."

Here is a simple version of a covenant marriage: *I will keep my promise even if you don't, because I've made a vow to God, not just to you.*

This takes all excuses off the table. It's no longer about whether you, as my spouse, keep your word, because I have vowed to keep mine unconditionally.

As I declare my vows in our marriage ceremony, *"... for better or for worse; for richer, for poorer; in sickness and in health; to love and to cherish; from this day forward until death do us part,"* I pledge to keep my word. No matter what choices you make, I promise to keep my vow.

This can be a real challenge when things aren't going well, but a committed spouse can be the anchor during the storm that helps the other find his or her way back.

When conflicts arise in a covenant marriage, there is a stronger love that helps hold things together—the love of God that has been woven into the marriage.

The first step in having a covenant marriage is answering the question, *Do you have a relationship with God?*

If you desire a relationship with God, please see the section "How to Have a Relationship With God" on page 100.

A relationship with God allows us to pledge, "My covenant I will not break, nor alter the word that has gone out of My lips" (Psalm 89:34).

Is your marriage based on a contract or on a covenant?

CHAPTER 12

THE INTENTIONAL
HUSBAND AND WIFE

When it comes to being intentional as a husband or a wife, several words come to mind: Deliberate. Designed. Calculated. Premeditated.

These are all *intentional* words. Intentional is not just an action, it is a lifestyle.

THE INTENTIONAL HUSBAND

As husbands, we are the first line of defense and a safe place for them to land.

Being an intentional husband means you operate according to I Peter 3:7:

> "In the same way, you husbands must give honor to your wives. Treat your wife with understanding as you live together. She may be weaker than you are, but she is your equal partner in God's gift of new life. Treat her as you should so your prayers will not be hindered." (NLT)

As husbands, we have the mandate to understand our wives. The old adage, *You'll never understand a woman,* isn't really true. Logic tells us that God will never direct us to do something He knows we can't do. It is true, however, that we probably can't understand our wives without His help.

Understanding our wives begins with the admission that we don't have all the answers. Thankfully, we can ask God to give us insight into the wives He's given us. As we faithfully seek God's counsel we'll do our parts. This includes taking time to understand our wives by studying them. As we study them, we'll begin to unravel the great mystery of understanding them.

Our mission involves three things: to protect, to provide, and to pursue.

PROTECT

It's important for husbands to understand their positions as their wives' protectors. This doesn't mean our wives are incapable of taking care of themselves. It means that we take our places as the heads of our wives (Eph. 5:23 NLT) by putting ourselves between them and the enemy. This might mean praying for them or praying with them. Sometimes it means letting them know we would give our lives to protect them.

This protection means we will not allow anyone to disrespect them. Sometimes this protection causes us to take the form of a proactive pray-er. As men of God, we have discernment. If we discern a possible danger or threat to our wives, we can invoke our authority as their husbands and stand against the enemy.

We husbands are the first line of defense and a safe place for them to land. They should never hesitate to be vulnerable with us. They need to know with certainty that we will always have their backs and will always be their strong support in time of need. Our willingness to protect them against all threats—physical, emotional, or spiritual—gives our wives much needed security.

PROVIDE

The next intentional action we should take is to be their providers. I (Dennis) had one man try to convince me that according to Matthew 6:25, he didn't have to be concerned about providing for his wife and children. He used this scripture to justify not working a full time job. While there is no shame if our wives make more money than we do, it is shameful to expect our wives to shoulder

Being a good provider also means providing support, understanding, love, and encouragement to our wives.

93

the greatest financial burden so we can pursue pipe dreams that never come to fruition.

Only insecure men have problems with their wives being well-compensated for what they do. If we as husbands are doing what God has called us to do, and our wives agree, then we are walking in our positions as providers. This issue is not about comparison, but about husbands doing our parts.

Susan and I supported each other as we took turns going back to school to further our educations. At different times in our marriage, one of us worked full time while the other attended classes. These times of unequal labor were by mutual agreement for a specific length of time. Because we put limits on this arrangement, the one who was working didn't feel taken advantage of by the other.

Although we've talked primarily about financial provision, it's also crucial for husbands to provide more than just money. Being a good provider also means providing support, understanding, love, and encouragement.

PURSUE

Pursuing our wives is not a onetime strategy to win her hand; it's a lifestyle of courting and dating.

Husbands are called to pursue. We must pursue our relationships with God, our calling in life, and our relationships with our wives. A frequent cry in the hearts of the women I counsel is for their husbands to pursue them like they did before they were married.

Many guys feel that once they're married, they have arrived. Most wives feel hugely disappointed when their husbands stop pursuing them. They assumed their husbands would always be attentive, loving, and pursuing. Being pursued, in their minds, demonstrates that their husbands enjoy their company and want to spend time with them.

Pursuing our wives is not a onetime strategy to win her hand; it's a lifestyle of courting and dating that says to her, *You are worth pursuing.* It also says to her, *I may have you, but I still want you.*

94

THE INTENTIONAL WIFE

An intentional wife is a woman who knows the importance of taking care of herself first. Since the emphasis of this book is about being intentional in our relationship with each other, why is it so important for a wife to take care of herself first?

Many women are more intentional in their care of their husbands, children, and others, but will frequently neglect themselves. We find a good example of why it's important for a wife to take care of herself first in the instructions flight attendants give airline passengers before takeoff.

As the flight attendant reviews emergency procedures in the event of an in-flight crisis, she includes instructions for parents traveling with children: "Place the oxygen mask on yourself first," she says, "before placing the mask over your child's mouth and nose." If a parent puts a mask on the child first, she explains, there is a risk that the parent might pass out before they get their own oxygen mask on. This will leave their child unattended during the emergency.

What can wives glean from these instructions? It's important to be intentional about taking care of yourselves so you can better care for the needs of your families. Caring for yourselves involves getting adequate rest, nourishment, mental health breaks, and recreation.

When a woman takes care of herself, she's more inclined to feel good about herself, and this carries over into her marriage.

It's OK for husbands and children to take care of themselves for a time. With a little coaching, they can learn how to prepare a meal, wash clothes, and do other simple chores that will allow you to have some *me* time.

If you feel you *have* to do everything, I encourage you to visit with a counselor to discuss what appropriate boundaries are and if you have a tendency to obtain your sense of self-worth from what you do rather than from whom you are.

Taking good care of your family doesn't mean you have to be responsible for everything 24/7. A truly responsible mom knows how important it is for her children to grow, mature, and learn how to take care of themselves.

I (Dennis) frequently encourage my wife to have some girl time with friends. I know how important it is for Susan to have fellowship and friendships with other women. When she's able to break away from her daily routine and hang out with other women, she comes home refreshed and recharged.

When a woman takes care of herself, she's more inclined to feel good about herself, and this carries over into her marriage. This doesn't just happen, however. It must be an intentional lifestyle choice.

Intentional wives are also purposeful about their relationships with their husbands. Speaking from a man's perspective, I (Dennis) know that it's very important for a husband to feel respected by his wife. One of the greatest gifts you can give your husband is to respect him. This can be especially challenging, however, when your husband hasn't given you much reason to respect him. In your frustration, you may feel you have no other options than to nag, yell, or scream. These behaviors, I assure you, won't produce the results you desire.

I suggest you try this strategy instead. Treat your husband today as the kind of husband you want him to be one day. It's amazing how a man responds to this kind of attention. Men often realize they don't deserve this kind of respect and will step up their game in response.

It's also important to pray intentionally for your husband to be the man God wants him to be. God can do in a moment what you cannot do in a lifetime. Sometimes this moment may happen immediately, other times change may begin, but take months or years to fully happen. Either way, I Peter 3:1-2 reminds us, "Then, even if some (husbands) refuse to obey the Good News, your godly lives will speak to them without any words. They will be won over by observing your pure and reverent lives" (NLT).

If you don't see changes right away, stay faithful, hopeful, and prayerful.

Treat your husband today as the kind of husband you want him to be one day.

FINAL THOUGHTS

Pursuing an intentional marriage is work—that four-letter word some of us try to avoid. But if both parties agree to be intentional about their marriage, good things will happen. Being intentional is choosing a deliberate lifestyle, not just administering a shot in the arm when things go badly.

If you read this book just to pacify your spouse, you may be wasting your time. If you read this with the intention of improving your relationship, you will see results.

This book is not a Band-Aid; it's a process to take your marriage to a new level. Susan and I encourage you to use this book as you would any tool—refer to it often, study the principles, and make time to read and discuss it with your spouse.

A counselor once posed this question to us years ago: "What if I told you that your marriage can be better than it ever was?" We were in a broken place and could hardly wrap our brains around that question. We can now say with confidence that our marriage is better than it ever was before, and yours can be, too. If what you've been doing isn't working, try something different. Why not make a covenant today to develop an intentional marriage?

ABOUT THE AUTHORS

DENNIS WELLS, M.MIN, MA, LPC

Licensed Professional Counselor

Dennis is a Licensed Professional Counselor and the founder of Wellsprings Professional Counseling. He is a graduate of Liberty University (Master of Arts in Professional Counseling) and Southwestern Christian University (Master of Ministry). Dennis is licensed with the State of South Carolina to provide psychotherapy and counseling. He offers therapy for pre-marital and marital counseling, family and relationship issues, and life coaching. Dennis works frequently with career counseling, parenting and adolescent issues.

He also has many years of experience as a pastor, church planter, ministry consultant, and licensed financial advisor with several insurance and banking institutions. Dennis has been married to Susan Wells for over 30 years and together they have three grown children. He loves sports, music, and a good laugh.

SUSAN B. WELLS, MSPAS, PA-C

Certified Physician Assistant

Susan is a Physician Assistant with a local OB/GYN practice. She graduated in 2008 from the Medical University of South Carolina with a Master of Science in Physician Assistant Studies. Her experience in women's healthcare stems from years of working as a surgical technologist with several labor and delivery units around the state.

She is extremely passionate concerning women's healthcare, educating women in maintaining a healthy lifestyle, and empowering women to become all they're created by God to be. Formerly the director for a statewide intercessory prayer network, Susan has partnered with her husband in ministry for many years. She enjoys speaking to various groups about prayer, and physical and spiritual health and well-being. She also enjoyed, in a time long ago, home-schooling their three children, who are now adults.

HOW TO HAVE
A RELATIONSHIP
WITH GOD

RECOGNIZE

Recognize that you do not have a relationship with God.

God desires for us to have a relationship with Him. Because of the sin of the first man, Adam, God's original relationship with mankind was broken. We may think that being a good person is enough to restore this relationship, but no matter how good a life we live, we still fall miserably short of being a good person. Being a good person is not enough to establish a relationship with God, because we are all sinners. "No one does good, not a single one" (Psalms 53:3 NLT).

We can't become who we're supposed to be without Jesus Christ. God in his mercy and love chose to send His only son Jesus to be a sacrifice for our sins.

"For God loved the world so much that he gave his one and only Son, so that everyone who believes in him will not perish but have eternal life. God sent his Son into the world not to judge the world, but to save the world through him" (John 3:16-17 NLT).

This is the Good News—that God loves us so much He sent His only Son—to die in our place—when we least deserved it.

REPENT

"Now repent of your sins and turn to God, so that your sins may be wiped away" (Acts 3:19 NLT).

The word *repent* means to turn away or change our direction. Instead of running from God, we can run to Him.

BELIEVE

Becoming a Christian doesn't mean just believing some creed or going to church; a Christian believes Jesus died for our sins.

> *"If you confess with your mouth that Jesus is Lord and believe in your heart that God raised him from the dead, you will be saved"* (Romans 10:9 NLT).

Believing in the death and resurrection of Jesus restores our relationship with God.

BE BAPTIZED

> *"Peter replied, "Each of you must repent of your sins and turn to God, and be baptized in the name of Jesus Christ for the forgiveness of your sins. Then you will receive the gift of the Holy Spirit."* (Acts 2:38)

COMMIT

Commit to a body of believers who can be a source of encouragement, discipleship, and love in order to continue to grow as an individual and as a couple.

NOTES

CHAPTER 2

1 Strong, James. Strong's Exhaustive Concordance of the Bible, Updated and Expanded Edition. (Peabody: Hendrickson Publishing, Inc., 2007).

CHAPTER 3

1 Everett L., Jr. *Hope-Focused Marriage Counseling.* (Downers Grove: InterVarsity Press, 1999).

2 Gottman, J.M., Coan., Carrere, S., Swanson. C. Predicting Marital Happiness and Stability from Newlywed Interaction, *Journal of Marriage and Family,* 1998, 5-22.

3 Ibid.

4 Ibid.

5 Ibid.

CHAPTER 6

1 Strong, James. *Strong's Exhaustive Concordance of the Bible, Updated and Expanded Edition.* (Peabody: Hendrickson Publishing, Inc., 2007).

2 Bouchez, Collette. *Choosing a Weight Loss Buddy,* WebMD , http://www.webmd.com/diet/features/choosing-weight-loss-buddy (accessed September 9, 2013).

CHAPTER 7

1 Gottman, J.M., Coan., Carrere, S., Swanson. C. *Predicting Marital Happiness and Stability from Newlywed Interaction, Journal of Marriage and Family,* (1998) 5-22.

2 Dew, Jeffrey and Wilcox, W. Bradford. *Give and You Shall Receive? Generosity, Sacrifice, & Marital Quality* (December 8, 2011). National marriage Project Working Paper No. 11-1, http://dx.doi.org/10.2139/ssrn.1970016 (accessed September 9, 2013).

3 Chapman, Gary. *The Five Love Languages* (Chicago: Northfield Publishing, 2010), 15.

CHAPTER 8

1 Harley, William F. *Surviving An Affair* (Grand Rapids: Fleming H. Revell, 1998), 87.

2 Ibid., 139

3 Ibid.

4 Ibid., 140

5 Ibid.

6 Ibid., 139

7 Ibid.

8 Ibid

9 Ibid.

10 Ibid., 91

11 Ibid., 92.

12 Ibid., 110

13 Ibid., 111

14 American Psychological Association. *Multitasking: Switching Costs.* (2006) http://apa.org/research/action/multitask.aspx. (accessed Sept. 9, 2013).

15 Ibid., 105.

Each of you should give what you have decided in your heart to give, not reluctantly or under compulsion, for God loves a cheerful giver. (2 Corinthians 9:7, NIV)

Although some individuals have a strong preference for giving anonymously, others believe that by making known their involvement, more individuals can be inspired to give. A friend of mine calls this "tithing your influence."

The truth is, motives for generous giving range from selfless to totally self-serving, and everywhere in between. While meditating on this wild assortment of reasons for giving can help us in our charitable work and as we ponder how to encourage more people to "get in the game," we can't afford to forget the most important question of all:

Why do **I** *want to get involved in philanthropy? What are* **my** *reasons for giving?*

Generosity Is the Thing

On one level, I suppose it doesn't make much of a difference why you want to "get in the game." The world and its people need help, and you've been granted the opportunity to give. In one way, a dollar given selfishly is no different than a dollar given selflessly; they'll both buy someone a dollar's worth of help.

In another way, though, it matters a great deal why you give. A selfish person rarely gives generously, and generosity is the thing I'm trying to encourage. I did not set out to write a book called *A Journey Toward Selfish Generosity.*

So . . . why do *you* give?

I think it's important that you know, because the answer will shape the rest of your journey. It will influence and even determine the kind

of generosity you express with your life. I want to promote smarter generosity, and the *why* greatly influences how smart we can become.

As I wrap up this little book, I am not going to sermonize. I am not going to lecture. I won't warn, chide, plead, flatter, wheedle, cajole, admonish or argue. I'm just going to follow the lead of my boss, who often ended His presentations with a question hanging in the air. So, here's my question:

Why do *you* give?

Appendix A

Recommended Reading

Brest, Paul and Hal Harvey. (2008.) *Money Well Spent: A Strategic Plan for Smart Philanthropy.* Bloomberg Press.

Buzzotta, Lefton, Cheney and Beatty. (1998). *Making Common Sense Common Practice.* New York: Psychological Associates Inc.

Callahan, David and Alfred A. Knoff. (2017). *The Givers: Wealth, Power, and Philanthropy in a New Gilded Age.* New York: Penguin Random House.

Corbett, Steve and Brian Fickert. (2014). *When Helping Hurts: How to Alleviate Poverty without Hurting the Poor…and Yourself.* Chicago: Moody Publishers.

George, Bill. (2003). *Authentic Leadership*. San Francisco: Jossey Bass.

Hybels, Bill. (2008). *Holy Discontent: Fueling the Fire that Ignites Personal Vision*. Grand Rapids: Zondervan.

Jernigan, Don. (2016). *The Hidden Power of Relentless Stewardship: 5 Keys to Developing a World-Class Organization*. New York: Rosetta Books.

Livermore, David A. (2012). *Serving with Eyes Wide Open: Doing Worldwide Missions with Cultural Intelligence*. Ada, MI: Baker Book House.

Lupton, Robert (2011). *Toxic Charity: How Churches and Charities Hurt Those They Help, and How to Reverse It*. New York: HarperCollins Books.

Macaulay, David (1988). *The Way Things Work*. Boston: Houghton Mifflin.

Macaulay, David (2016). *The Way Things Work Now*. Boston: Houghton Mifflin Harcourt and Dorling Kindserley.

Stern, Kenneth (2013). *With Charity for All: Why Charities are Failing and a Better Way to Give*. New York: Doubleday.

Townsend, John (2018). *Leading from Your Gut*. Grand Rapids: Zondervan.

Appendix B

Popular Giving Vehicles

A comparison of donor-advised funds, supporting organizations, and private foundations

ISSUE / FEATURE	DONOR-ADVISED FUNDS	SUPPORTING ORGANIZATIONS	PRIVATE FOUNDATIONS
Description of the giver's role and Governance	Givers have advisory privileges only. Ultimate control rests with the public charity.	Neither the giver nor a family member can control, directly or indirectly, more than 49% of the board, but the giver may participate in the selection of board members.	The giver family can control 100% of the board; however, after the giver's death, the board has control.
Control over grants and assets	The giver may recommend grants and investment options, but the public charity has ultimate control over decisions.	The giver may recommend grants and investments, but the board of the SO has ultimate control over decisions.	The board has complete control of all grants and investment decisions, subject to self-dealing rules.
Tax deduction limits for gifts of cash and publicly-traded securities	Cash: 60% of adjusted gross income; publicly-traded securities: 30% of adjusted gross income	Cash: 60% of adjusted gross income; publicly-traded securities: 30% of adjusted gross income	Cash: 30% of adjusted gross income; publicly-traded securities: 20% of adjusted gross income
Tax deduction limits for other non-liquid appreciated assets (long-term capital gain)	Fair market value up to 30% of adjusted gross income	Fair market value up to 30% of adjusted gross income	Lesser of fair market value or the giver's basis in asset up to 20% of adjusted gross income
Investment excise taxes	None	None	Must pay tax on investment income
Distribution requirements	None	None	5% of foundation assets must be distributed annually
Start-up costs[1]	None	Legal and state fees for incorporation, IRS filing, and other documents (no IRS filing if under NCF group exemption)	Legal and state fees for incorporation, IRS filing, and other documents
Ongoing administrative and management costs[1]	It varies depending on the public charity providing the service ... generally 1% per year or less.	Ongoing fees for accounting, legal, and administrative advisors to oversee the assets, balance the books, pay the bills, keep the records, and file the tax returns	Ongoing fees for accounting, legal, and administrative advisors to oversee the assets, balance the books, pay the bills, keep the records, and file the tax returns
Ability to employ people and pay salaries and benefits	No	Yes, subject to reasonable compensation limits; no to substantial contributors[2]	Yes, subject to reasonable compensation limits
Ability to pay expenses for travel/other reimbursements	No	Yes, able to pay expenses but not able to reimburse expenses to substantial contributors[2]	Yes
Ability to make grants to non-exempt individuals	No	Yes, subject to the same requirements as grants to foreign charitable organizations	Yes, subject to the same requirements as grants to foreign charitable organizations
Anonymity of giver	Yes	No[3]	No[3]
Privacy	Complete privacy is available. DAF information is aggregated with other DAF information to maintain privacy, and an individual tax return is not required for each DAF.	The entity must file Form 990, which becomes a matter of public record and contains detailed information on grants, investment fees, salaries, etc.[3]	The entity must file Form 990 which becomes a matter of public record and contains detailed information on grants, investment fees, salaries, etc.[3]
Succession and Perpetuity	Can exist in perpetuity	Can exist in perpetuity	Can exist in perpetuity

1. The creation of any legal entity, especially one that could last in perpetuity and/or involves irrevocable actions, requires the careful input and oversight of a competent attorney that has a thorough understanding of the giver's family and their giving goals and objectives.

2. Substantial contributors are defined in IRC § 507(d)(2)(A).

3. Combining this tool with a donor-advised fund (NCF Giving Fund) can achieve partial privacy and anonymity.

* Information in this chart is based on federal laws as of the date of this printing. These laws are subject to change and can affect the accuracy of this information.

Appendix C

Questions to Help You on Your Way

If you would like a little "boost" on your way to discovering where you might realize the biggest impact in your life of philanthropy, the following questions may be helpful to you. I have organized the questions that follow into six broad categories:

- ➤ Background
- ➤ Gifting
- ➤ Training
- ➤ Interests
- ➤ Goals
- ➤ Calling

While most of these categories have some connection with one another, they also differ from each other in significant ways. By the time you finish reflecting upon and answering these questions, I hope you will find yourself better equipped to start walking down a smarter path to a life of generosity.

Your Background

1. Describe the home in which you grew up. What "life lessons" did you learn there?

2. Who were your three best friends as a child? As a teen? What drew you to them?

3. Where did you experience the most success as a child? As an adolescent? As a young adult?

4. What shaped you the most in your formative years? Who had the greatest influence on you? Why?

5. Pick a single word to describe your background. Why did you choose this word?

6. Describe the single greatest experience of your life so far. What made this experience "great"?

7. Describe the single worst or hardest experience of your life so far. Why was it so difficult for you?

8. What do you value most about your background? What do you value least? Why?

9. Name a teacher who had a strong influence or effect on you, whether good or bad. How does that teacher's influence continue to influence you now?

10. If you had a time machine and could return to any moment in your life—but only as an observer—to what moment in your past would you return? Why?

Your Gifting

1. Name what you consider to be your three top gifts, strengths, talents or traits. Where do you shine?

2. Ask the person closest to you—your spouse, friend, co-worker, family member—to identify what he or she views as your top three gifts. (No coaching!) Do your lists match? Are they close? What can you glean from this comparison?

3. Describe the sense of pleasure or satisfaction you get from using

your top three gifts.

4. What have these gifs enabled you to accomplish so far?

5. How do others tend to rely on your gifts? What are you often asked to do?

6. Name the two or three most memorable compliments you have received from people who praised you for using your gifts effectively.

7. Think of a time or place when you wanted to use your gifts but couldn't. What stopped you? How did that experience make you feel?

8. Think about the future: Where and how would you like to use your gifts? (Don't limit your imagination!)

9. Think about how your gifts engage or connect well with the gifts of others. Where have you seen your gifts complement those of others? Where have you seen them clash with others?

10. How have you honed your gifts? Where do they still need more sharpening?

Your Training

1. What subjects did you like in school? What subjects did you hate? Why?

2. What special training have you received that continues to help you succeed?

3. In what areas of school did you excel? Where did you struggle?

4. If you attended college, what kind of training did you receive there? Have you remained in the field for which you trained? Why or why not? If you didn't attend college, name the most helpful training you received as a young adult. What made this training so exceptional?

5. Name an area in which you'd still like to get some training. Why do you want it? How might it help you? How could you get the training you desire? For what purpose would you use it?

6. What sort of training, formal or informal, has most helped you to succeed in your current career? What made this training so effective or helpful?

7. Describe your learning style. What helps you learn most effectively? How quickly do you learn? What kind of learning process is challenging for you? Do people generally like to have you as a student? Are you "teachable?" Explain or give examples.

8. Describe yourself as a trainer. Who have you trained? In what have you trained them? Do you think they learned well from you as a trainer? Did they enjoy learning from you? Explain.

9. Imagine yourself in ten years. How has your life training equipped you to be an effective philanthropist? Where might you still be struggling in a decade? What kind of training could you get today that could help you years from now?

Your Interests

1. List your five top interests in regard to your job or career.

2. List your five top interests that are *not* related to your work.

3. On your "average work day," which of your activities or responsibilities is most enjoyable or interesting to you? Why? Which activities do you enjoy the least? Why?

4. On your days off, what do you most enjoy doing, and why do you enjoy it?

5. Outside of your work, if you could spend a year doing one thing, what would it be? Why?

6. Do you enjoy reading? What do you like reading about in your spare time?

7. If you ran an international media conglomerate, what topics would you choose as your focus to highlight? Why?

8. Think of the most fulfilling moment you experienced in the past month. What were you doing? Why did you find the experience to be so fulfilling?

9. What causes you to smile, without fail? What gets your blood pumping (outside of exercise)? What would you give a million dollars to be a part of?

10. Describe your most common daydreams. What hopes or dreams just keep coming back to you?

Your Goals

1. What would you like to accomplish in the next five years?
2. What would you like to accomplish in the next ten years?
3. What do you hope to have accomplished by the end of your life?
4. Name a personal goal that you have yet to reach. What has kept you from reaching that goal?
5. Identify three purposes or goals that you'd like to accomplish through your philanthropy.
6. Name a career goal that you seem close to reaching. How did you get to this point?
7. Maybe, like Steve, you tend to have more "directions" than "goals." What current directions interest you the most? Why?
8. Think about the kind of philanthropy you *might* want to pursue. Identify one short-term goal (within one month), a medium-term goal (within six months) and a long-term goal (within one year) that could help you to determine what kind of projects or needs you'd like to learn more about or pursue.
9. Whom do you know who actively pursues some philanthropic interests? Invite the person out for coffee, explaining that you'd like to learn about his or her goals for giving. What, specifically, do they want to accomplish through their philanthropy?
10. Describe your current overall goal for your giving, regardless of how formed or unformed it might be. What would you like to accomplish?

Your Calling

1. A calling can be described as a strong desire for a particular way of life or vocation. What does "calling" mean to you?

2. A "calling" implies being chosen or requested by someone, a value or some force. If you believe you have a calling, who is the one, force, or value that is calling you? Explain.

3. Do you believe you have a philanthropic "calling"? If so, what is it? If not, do you wish you had one? Explain.

4. Interview someone you know who has mentioned their own "calling." Find out all you can about this calling: What it is, how they got or discovered it, how it motivates them, whether it grows or changes, how it helps them direct their activities, etc.

5. Consider reading the book *The Call: Finding and Fulfilling the Central Purpose of Your Life,* by Os Guinness (2003). If you read the book, describe your chief take-away from it.

6. How do you believe a clear sense of a personal calling would benefit you as you pursue a life of generosity?

7. The Bible frequently uses the word "calling" ("called," "calls") to speak about God's plans for a person's life. Describe what the following New Testament text means to you:

   ". . . we constantly pray for you, that our God may make you worthy of his calling, and that by his power he may bring to fruition your every desire for goodness and your every deed prompted by faith" (2 Thessalonians 1:11).

8. Describe what the following quote by Charles Swindoll means to you:

   "When you have a sense of calling, whether it's to be a musician, soloist, artist, in one of the technical fields, or a plumber, there is something deep and enriching when you realize it isn't just a casual choice, it's a divine calling."[37]

9. How would a sense of "calling" affect the application of the following quote by Bill Gates?

> "Effective philanthropy requires a lot of time and creativity—the same kind of focus and skills that building a business requires."[38]

10. Invest some time in thinking about your own calling, its nature or even its possibility. Then, in the space below, write a concise statement of your personal calling—or if you're not sure you have one, a concise statement of what a personal calling for you *might* look like:

Once you've worked through all of the preceding questions (and a few exercises), try to synthesize your answers into a brief, working statement of who you are. Write that statement below.

This is who I am:

Now, here's the *vital* question: What might a life of generosity look like for a person who describes him/herself as you have just written? Where could such a person most satisfyingly begin to walk a journey of smarter philanthropy?

That is the chapter you need to write.
Start *today.*

Endnotes

1 Gates, Mary. "Bill Gates' mother inspired philanthropy." Business Insider, 10 May 2015. https://www.businessinsider.com/bill-gates-mother-inspired-philanthropy-2015-5/?r=SPH&IR=T. Accessed 13 Nov 2018.

2 "benchmarking." *BusinessDictionary,* 5 Dec. 2018, http://www.businessdictionary.com/definition/benchmarking.html.

3, Ben Bloch, "Chip Kelly takes the fast track to tremendous heights at Oregon before hitting speed bumps in the NFL."

4. Bill George, *Authentic Leadership* (San Francisco: Jossey Bass, 2003), 63.

5. "Pursuing your Philanthropic Vision." US Trust, www.ustrust.com/articles/pursuing-your-philanthropic-vision.html.

6. Don Jernigan, *The Hidden Power of Relentless Stewardship: 5 Keys to Developing a World-Class Organization* (New York: Rosetta Books, 2016), 74.

7. Buzzotta, Lefton, Cheney and Beatty. *Making Common Sense Common Practice.* New York: Psychological Associates Inc., 1998.

8. Rita Gunther McGrath and Ian MacMillan, "Discovery-Driven Planning," *Harvard Business Review,* July-August 1995.

9. "Peter Principle." *Investopedia.com.* https://www.investopedia.com/terms/p/peter-principle.asp. Accessed Nov 26, 2018.

10. Lupton, Robert D. *Toxic Charity: How Churches and Charities Hurt Those They Help (And How to Reverse It).* Harper Collins Publishers, 2002.

11. Livermore, David. *Serving with Eyes Wide Open.* Baker Publishing Group, 2012.

12. Fikkert, Brian and Steve Corbett. *When Helping Hurts: Alleviating Poverty without Hurting the Poor—and Yourself.* Moody Publishers, 2009.

13. Lupton, Robert. *Charity Detox: What Charity Would Look Like if We Cared about Results.* HarperOne, 2015. Moody Publishers, 2009.

14. Minnesota Multiphasic Personality Inventory. https://www.verywellmind.com/what-is-the-minnesota-multiphasic-personality-inventory-2795582

15. https://en.wikipedia.org/wiki/Myers%E2%80%93Briggs_Type_Indicator

16. https://en.wikipedia.org/wiki/DISC_assessment

17. ttps://en.wikipedia.org/wiki/Big_Five_personality_traits

18. https://consciousendeavors.org/core-values-index/

19. Adam Baum, "Xavier basketball grad transfer Zach Hankins: 'I never thought I'd get here.'" Sept. 21, 2018. https://www.cincinnati.com/story/sports/college/xavier/xaviersports/2018/09/21/xavier-basketball-grad-transfer-zach-hankins-never-thought-id-get-here/1344484002/

20. Hybels, Bill. *Holy Discontent: Fueling the Fire that Ignites Personal Vision.* Zondervan, 2008.

21. Collins, Jim. https://www.jimcollins.com/concepts/bhag.html

22. https://www.goodreads.com/quotes/6946-not-all-of-us-can-do-great-things-but-we

23. Accidental Creative. "Finding Your Sweet Spot." Todd Henry. https://www.accidentalcreative.com/creating/why-you-need-tour-sweet-spot/

24. Townsend, John *Leading from Your Gut.* Zondervan: 2018.

25. Buechner, Frederick. *Wishful Thinking* (New York: Harper & Row, 1973), 118-119.

26. https://www.independent.co.uk/news/world/americas/america-new-zealand-and-canada-top-list-of-world-s-most-generous-nations-a6849221.html

27. "Highlights: An overview of giving in 2017," Giving USA 2018.

28. Alix Spiegel, "Why Do We Give? Not Why Or How You Think," npr.com, November 25, 2011.

29. Spiegel.

30. Spiegel.

31. Spiegel.

32. Phyllis Korkki, "Why do people donate to charity?" *The New York Times,* December 22, 2013.

33. Michael Sanders and Francesca Tamma, "The science behind why people give to charity." *The Guardian,* US edition, March 23, 2015.

34. Sanders and Tamma.

35. Sanders and Tamma.

36. https://www.networkforgood.com/nonprofitblog/how-to-get-donations-14-reasons-why-people-donate/

37. Swindoll, Charles. https://www.brainyquote.com/quotes/charles_r_swindoll_578725

38. Gates, Bill. https://www.brainyquote.com/quotes/bill_gates_626084

Made in the
USA
Lexington, KY

Made in the USA
Middletown, DE
31 May 2015